The Diary of Bishop Edward Feild in 1844

The Diary of Bishop Edward Feild in 1844

Edited by Ronald Rompkey

Cover photo of Bishop field courtesy of Queen's College Archives.

ISER Books gratefully acknowledges the support of the Faculty of Arts, Memorial University of Newfoundland.

Library and Archives Canada Cataloguing in Publication

Feild, Edward, 1801-1876
The diary of Bishop Edward Feild in 1844 / edited by Ronald Rompkey.

(Social and economic studies ; 73)
Includes bibliographical references.
ISBN 978-1-894725-10-1

1. Feild, Edward, 1801-1876 — Diaries. 2. United Church of England and Ireland. Diocese of Newfoundland — History. 3. Church of England. Diocese of Newfoundland — History. 4. Church of England — Newfoundland and Labrador — History — 19th century. 5. Newfoundland and Labrador — Description and travel. 6. Church of England — Bishops — Diaries. 7. Bishops — Newfoundland and Labrador — Diaries. I. Rompkey, Ronald II. Title. III. Series: Social and economic studies (St. John's, N.L.)

BX5620.F53.A3 2010 283.092 C2010-905465-2

Published by ISER Books — Faculty of Arts Publications
Institute of Social and Economic Research
Memorial University of Newfoundland
297 Mount Scio Road
St. John's, NL A1C 5S7

www.arts.mun.ca/iserbooks

Printed and bound in Canada

Preface

The diary of Edward Feild, second Anglican Bishop of Newfoundland, provides the new bishop's private reflections upon leaving his home in England and travelling for the first time to North America. Apart from any apprehensions he expresses about his new mission in life, we find him preoccupied not only with Christian education but with the arrangement of church buildings and church ritual as it was practised in the colonies, as well as with the need for building in St. John's a cathedral, for which the foundation stone had been laid in 1843. The diary gives us insights into his thoughts as a Tractarian — a follower of the Oxford Movement, begun in 1833 by clergy at Oxford University to renew the Church of England by reviving Catholic doctrines and rituals. I am grateful to the McCord Museum for permission to publish the diary as it appears in MS M2297.

More particular details concerning Feild's plans for a cathedral are shown in his correspondence with the Rev. William Scott and the report of the Cathedral Building Committee. I am grateful to the Bishop of Eastern Newfoundland and Labrador, the Rt. Rev. Cyrus Pitman, for permission to publish these letters, and to my colleague, Professor Shane O'Dea, for the use of an earlier transcription. We can observe in Feild's diary and letters, after his travelling throughout his new diocese and observing what he calls "a pretty colonial mess," that he felt compelled to lay out what he viewed as the orthodoxy of church services; and his charge to the clergy in 1844 is an unreserved corrective to the kinds of variants he had found.

Bishop Feild's diary consists of 250 pages of text written in a parenthetical and allusive style, beginning with his consecration on 28 April 1844. Prior to his departure on 4 June, the diary records social and ecclesiastical events and daily habits, and these have been excluded from the present volume. Because the circumstances of composition did not allow the bishop sufficient leisure for careful writing and editing, certain passages are difficult to read, if not illegible. I have endeavoured, as far as possible, to represent both diary and letters precisely, but where it has not been possible, I have offered an interpretation or an ellipsis in square brackets. Punctuation and paragraphing also have been altered and the spelling corrected or modernized for the sake of clarity.

Contents

Introduction

To the Anglican Church in Newfoundland and Labrador, Bishop Edward Feild stands as an intrepid figure, who both intellectually and physically shaped his diocese with such force that the fruits of his labours can be seen to this day. In addition to the hagiography and encomia accorded him since his death, for decades the boys of Bishop Feild College have extolled his virtues in a school song that begins,

> In Terra Nova's capital our fabric proudly stands,
> A monument to him whose name it bears;
> 'Twas his to be a champion of piety and truth,
> To grapple like a giant with the ignorance of youth.

This last phrase acknowledges not only Feild's episcopal influence but his innovations as an educator, the one who laid the foundations for Newfoundland's denominational school system and the training of its clergy. Legends of Feild's exceptional efforts abound, together with his own published accounts of travels throughout his diocese; but insights into his private thinking exist only in unpublished diaries and correspondence, the most revealing of which is the present diary chronicling his first months in office, preserved at the McCord Museum in Montreal. In this diary, which begins after his ordination by the Archbishop of Canterbury in April 1844 and ends in August of the same year, we are offered a rare glimpse of his habits of mind.

Feild was born in 1801, the son of a Worcester surgeon. After finishing his secondary education at Rugby School, he took a degree at Oxford at the age of 22, then a master's in mathematics and classics. Gifted with a robust constitution, he was also a competent athlete, sailor, and horseman. At Queen's College Oxford, he became a devoted High Churchman and educationist, twin preoccupations whose significance became evident from the start of his career. Ordained a priest in 1827, he began his ministry as curate of the parish of Kidlington, Oxfordshire, and built a school there. In 1833, as rector of English Bicknor, Gloucestershire, situated on the banks of the Wye, he again distinguished himself as an advocate of educational reform. Recognized by then as a force in educational policy, he was made the first inspector of the church's National School Society in 1839 and in this capacity occupied himself not only with the curriculum but also with the recruitment of teachers, discipline, finances, and buildings.

When Aubrey Spencer, Newfoundland's first Anglican bishop (with jurisdiction in Bermuda), was forced to resign because of ill-health after only four years, Feild, with his hardy constitution and his experience in embattled parishes where he had confronted ignorance, poverty, and drunkenness, was a prime candidate to succeed him. Consecrated bishop on 28 April 1844, he was made inspector of the Newfoundland School Society as well. Consequently, as a Tractarian, he proceeded to change not only the ritualistic style of his diocese but the internal arrangement of its churches despite the resistance of evangelicals. Tractarianism was a movement in the Church of England that developed into Anglo-Catholicism, its members promoting the reinstatement of certain Catholic doctrines and rituals. The term "Tractarian" is associated further with a series of publications, *Tracts for the Times*, published from 1833 to 1841. Two of the prominent Tractarians were John Henry Newman and Edward Bouverie Pusey. Others included John Keble, Charles Marriott, Richard Hurrell Froude, Robert Wilberforce, Isaac Williams, and William Palmer. Feild carried the ideas of such men with him as he travelled the island colony's outports by sea — even to Labrador — and increased the number of clergy from 12 to 50. The founder of Queen's Theological College, he also began construction of a neo-gothic cathedral and the development of a state-supported denominational school system. After wielding his authority for 32 years, he resigned in 1876 because of ill-health and died shortly thereafter in Hamilton, Bermuda, where he is buried.

Feild's diary, which begins in this edition with his voyage to North America, includes a two-week sojourn in Halifax, where in company with his assistant, the Rev. Charles Palairet, he consulted with the Bishop of Nova Scotia, John Inglis, and awaited transport to St. John's. During this interval, he was introduced to the idiosyncrasies of the colonial church and the system of colonial government with which he would struggle throughout the years to come. As a Tractarian, he was especially apt to comment on the behaviour of clergy and the internal arrangement of churches. But that is not all. He let nothing escape his gaze, and he presents an exceptionally detailed description of the town of Halifax, the varieties of tree and plant life, and the weather. During a short trip to Windsor, Nova Scotia, he presents an evaluation of King's College, an exceptional glimpse of the educational environment and architectural layout of that institution. Bishop Inglis wrote the Society for the Propagation of the Gospel on Feild's departure,

> Surely it is time for me to name my dear Brother of Newfoundland. His arrival and his stay for a fortnight have been a delight to me, and his departure yesterday, just as your letter arrived, was full of sorrow. He appears to be pureminded and singlehearted in an eminent degree, and these qualifications will help him continually. He has not left Bicknor without a struggle, but I have encouraged him in the path ahead, which may sometimes be rough. I accompanied him to Windsor, and

> he visited all things at the College, the School, and the Church there. Here he has visited the National, the African and Sunday Schools. He preached twice in St. Paul's, once in St. George's and also once at Dartmouth. I have assured him of my desire to make the experience of my grey hairs useful to him at all times, if he need help. He had no time to reply to your letter yesterday, but he asked me to give you the names of a few persons he hopes to employ.[1]

In addition to his Tractarian Anglo-Catholicism, Feild's diary is an example of what is now recognized as the rhetoric of empire, a mode of expression found in travel writing such as his. The rhetoric of empire consists of literary conventions that confirm imperial authority through an assumed dominion or sovereignty. And since Nova Scotia and Newfoundland were both colonies at the time, Feild's rhetoric falls into the same category as that of other colonial administrators, a category whereby one culture not only dominates another but interprets it through the hegemonic force of ideas. Within the colonial discourse, observers typically fix upon the physical landscape as part of their interest in natural history, but at the same time they see the lives of local people as extensions of that landscape. In this way, Feild is almost always judgemental, and his observations are sometimes fraught with condescension.

The kind of reporting expressed through colonial discourse begins with the privilege of inspecting and examining. A further trope is the alignment of local landscapes and geographical features with features in the home country, a form of appropriation that takes the home country as the norm. It is also apt to classify non-European groups such as blacks and Aboriginals according to their perceived degree of sophistication. And since classification is never completely free of evaluation, here it is implied (if not always expressed) that colonials and native people are inferior. Within the same discourse, colonial space is often characterized as empty, as if nothing has happened within it, and this is shown by singling out the lack of cultivation and the absence of abundant natural growth commonly found in England. These and other tropes find their way into Feild's journal as he is introduced to the landscape and the people of Nova Scotia and Newfoundland. On the surface, he may seem merely to describe, but his gaze is the gaze of the colonizer and his discourse the discourse of numerous travellers, officers, and administrators who have carried out their duties through the British Empire.

[1]SPG Records, Oxford, MG1, vol. 482, letter 297: Inglis to SPG, 2 July 1844.

1. Liverpool to Halifax: Visit to Windsor

Tuesday, June 4

At 9 o'clock went down to St. Martin's Church to receive the Holy Sacrament with several of the clergy of Liverpool and others, about 12 or 14 clergymen besides Rev. E. Hawkins[2] and Rev. C. Palairet, my brother also and perhaps 30 lay people. After this service I proceeded with Mr. Wray to the Church of St. Nicholas (Mr. Campbell), where their clergy were assembled. We went thence in procession to the quay, I taking Mr Campbell's arm and the clergy following two and two — at the steps of the quay Mr Campbell made a short address in the name of the clergy of Liverpool, wishing me God speed in my great undertaking. I shook hands with each of the clergy, who then departed to attend the Bishop of Chester's visitation.

At eleven o'clock I went on board the tender with Revd. E. Hawkins & Mrs. Wray and presently proceeded to the *Acadia*, which lay a short distance off in the Mersey. My brother & Palairet were a few minutes too late to go with us in the tender, but they followed with the mailbags, which came off about 12½ o'clock. Immediately on their arrival we weighed anchor. My brother, Mr. Wray and Revd. E. Hawkins, with others, returned in the mailboat to the shores after a sad farewell, and I and Palairet were carried away and away. Little did it betide us to wave our handkerchiefs and kiss our hands, farther and farther were we carried out and away, till in the smoke from the firing of a salute by our ship I lost sight altogether of my last friend who had continued with me, except faithful Palairet was alone in the wide world on the wild sea.

We were each too much taken up with the thoughts of those whom we had left and lost to consider much the single one that remained. Never before did I look upon a parasol with interest, but what would I not have given to have been under or near that light blue one which I knew to be in Mrs. Wray's hand, and near which I knew also were my dear brother and my dear friend E. Hawkins. We went easily and quickly down the river — but before night the wind began to get round to the West. The last land I saw was in the evening of this day off Holyhead, whence I saw a steamer was stretching out for Dublin. The evening closed in and I went to bed sad and sorrowful enough, but still hoping that I had been guided aright and therefore

[2]Rev. Ernest Hawkins, Secretary of the Society for the Propagation of the Gospel.

putting my trust in the Lord and committing my way unto Him, beseeching Him to prosper it to His own glory and the good of His church, whether my portion should be joy or sorrow, honour or shame, in whatever manner He might be pleased to deal with me.

Wednesday, June 5

I arose first and jumping out of the upper cot sorely hurt my foot. I was soon slightly seasick. I contrived how to shave. Palairet rose after me but did not attempt the shaving process. The day became wet, upon which we congratulated our friends in England more than ourselves. The wind freshening also from the West, the sea broke against us and the vessel pitched a good deal, and almost all the passengers became sick. I suffered among the rest, but Palairet much more. He took nothing all day. The day was in all respects miserable, but except inwardly I did not suffer so much as many of my fellow steam-travellers — or indeed as near — I slept a little during the day.

Thursday, June 6

Palairet arose first, having gone to bed quite early the night before — I had slept but little. I got out my cot cautiously and safely, taking firm hold of a brass hook on which I had hung my hat. I was sick immediately after getting up, but not again during the day, but exceedingly uncomfortable, as were most of the passengers. Palairet continued very unwell and took nothing. I was quite unable to do any business — and almost to think about my state, which however I felt to be forlorn and desolate enough.

Friday, June 7

This is my [43rd] birthday, though there is none to tell me so. How shall I keep it? In "double pomp of sadness"?[3] as being the most gloomy and desolate, the most full of dreary and direful anticipations and the most forsaken of friends and all earthly comforts of any and all I have yet in my life seen? or in humble joy and thankfulness that I have been raised, all unworthy, to an office of great dignity and usefulness in the Church and have been just set forward in a course which, if zealously and faithfully pursued, may be blessed to the good of Christ's holy church and my own salvation. Either way and every way this is and deserves to be considered by far the most important day and crisis of my life — the birthday of many new hopes and fears — of joy and reward if I have grace to be faithful in my sacred calling and un-

[3]John Dryden, *All for Love* (1677), 1.1.222-24: Marc Antony. They tell me 'tis my birthday, and I'll keep it/With double pomp of sadness./'Tis what the day deserves, which gave me breath.

dertaking, but of shame and sorrow forever if I receive this grace of God in vain, if I faint and look back having not put my hand to the plough.[4]

I used years ago to think that I should like to be a bishop at or about 40 years of age, hoping and thinking I might by that time prepare myself, as far as study and experience and reflection could prepare me for the duties and responsibilities of that office. Now I find that I have not in fact made any of that preparation I had intended and expected, and I feel that at least as many more years would be required to make it — rather that it is an office far too sacred, high and difficult for me, and yet, trusting in God that He has some good and gracious purpose in calling me to it, I have dared to accept it. All I ask is to be pardoned myself and that God may be honoured whether by my life or death, sorrow or joy, honour or shame. Amen.

Saturday, June 8

I took occasion this day to look round me a little on my ship and shipmates. The good ship *Acadia* is one of the British and North American Royal Mail steam packets maintained by the British government for the conveyance of the mails to and from the North American colonies and the United States (612 tons new measurement) 1200 tons old measure and 440 horsepower. These packets sail twice a month (i.e., the 4th and 19th of each month from Liverpool and the 1st and 15th of each month from Boston). They call at Halifax both going and returning. The voyage from Liverpool to Halifax averages 12 days and from Halifax to Liverpool 10 days. The *Acadia* is a very clean, tight, well-appointed ship. The saloon is a large, long room on the deck where the passengers take their meals at 2 long tables.

The staterooms or sleeping berths are below: each stateroom contains two berths, which are little drawers or shelves just large enough to receive your body but will hardly contain your mind if it be a big or roaming one. One berth is just over the other, and it requires some little dexterity and strength to get in and yet more to get out of the upper one. It is quite necessary in getting out to have firm hold of a hook or string with your hand and so to step down (not jump) by help of the seat. For want of this knowledge and precaution, the first morning I seriously hurt my foot and otherwise discomposed myself body and mind — my partner or chum in the stateroom was my friend Palairet. I being the more aspiring and adventurous of the two took the upper berth. The upper berth has perhaps most air, but it has also much the most rolling and noise. The creaking of the timbers resembles that of a 100 pairs of Mr. Terrett's new boots, and when the ship rolls or tosses is incessant and drives away all sleep.

The rolling also is at first very unpleasant and occasions some apprehensions of falling out and tends to seasickness. The bad effects of the rolling, however, are

[4]Luke 9: 62: And Jesus said unto him, No man, having put his hand to the plough, and looking back, is fit for the kingdom of God.

soon got over. At first, "Dire was the tossing, deep the groans."[5] The stateroom occupied by myself and Palairet was numbered 57 and 58 and being near the centre of the vessel did not toss us about so much as those nearer the stern. It was also not on the outside of the vessel, so that we did not hear much of the waters — and being under the saloon we escaped also the noise the [holy time] in the morning which is heard distinctly in those berths immediately under the deck. I imagine, however, the creaking of the ship was louder here than in some other parts and was to me the greatest nuisance of all.

The berths are very small. There is a washing stand and small seat and drawer for each, but it would be almost impossible (if otherwise desirable) for two to dress or undress at the same time. Palairet generally went to bed very early and rose first. He slept well, but my rest was much broken. On the other hand, after the 2nd day, he was well during the daytime, and he continued sick and weak for a full week, refusing to take food except once or twice a day and in very small quantities. I followed the course recommended of eating frequently and moderately and after Thursday morning suffered nothing from sickness. If my body had not been otherwise disordered by the excitement and fatigue and late hours of the last 3 weeks I might have benefited by the voyage. As it was, none of the functions were regular, and I had no enjoyment and little benefit from the voyage.

The cabin passengers were about 60 gentlemen and ladies. The ladies were (1) Mrs. Featherstonhaugh, the wife of the author of *Excursions in America*,[6] going to her family (her mother and sisters) near New York for her health, leaving her husband and 3 children in England; (2) Mrs. Forsythe, the wife of a Canadian gentleman returning from Scotland (from a visit to her mother) with her husband and two children; (3) Mrs. Macaulay returning with her husband from a tour in Europe to Canada; (4) a Spanish lady with her husband and 2 children; (5) a lady of New York with her husband, an agent of the steam packet company.

The gentlemen were (1) English — 2 officers going to join their regiments in Canada, Palairet and myself; (2) Canadian — Mr. Forsythe and Mr. Macaulay; (3) French — two or three; (4) Spanish — two; (5) Swiss — two; (6) American — about 40; (7) Irish — three or four. The Canadians were staunch Tories and Churchmen and seemed more suspicious of the Americans than even the English are. They do not like Lord Stanley[7] as colonial minister and report him as less Conservative

[5]John Milton, *Paradise Lost* (1674), 11: 489-90: Dire was the tossing, deep the groans, Despair/Tended the sick busiest from couch to couch.

[6]George William Featherstonhaugh, *Excursion Through the Slave States, from Washington to the Frontier of Mexico, With Sketches of Popular Manners and Geological Notices*, 2 vols. (London, 1844).

[7]Edward George Geoffrey Smith Stanley, 14th Earl of Derby (1799-1869), appointed Secretary of State for War and the Colonies in 1837.

than Lord John Russell.[8] They augur very ill of the prospects of the Canadas and think Sir C. Metcalfe[9] as come too late to save them from being swamped by the democratic party. The Swiss, Irish, Spanish, French and Americans seem chiefly engaged in trade.

The Americans are returning to their country after having made their purchases in England. They are chiefly young men, partners in large firms, and many of them go over to England and return every year. They seem men of good education and information (many of them speak two languages) and by no means inferior to men of their situation and circumstances in England in manners and behaviour. I was agreeably surprised to find very little smoking among them and almost no spitting or swearing. They readily enter into conversation and make themselves agreeable. They are very open in their discourse with each other about their affairs, and I should think cannot be close or covetous, though eager in the pursuit of money. They live plentifully and are well satisfied with their accommodation, their companions and themselves. There is no blustering or boasting among them.

There is one remarkable and disagreeable (at least to me) peculiarity in their appearance, which however, I believe, is copied from young France, viz., in their thick, bushy fringe of hair going from whisker to whisker under the chin. It reminds me of the hooded serpents I used to see when a boy in Salmon's modern history,[10] and to my eyes is exceedingly ugly. Some of them cherish mustachios also and generally have long locks behind which they cultivate with considerable care. Upon the whole, they are superior to my expectation in appearance, manners and attainments and above all civility. They are not unwilling to see advantages and blessings in England which can hardly be matched even in America. They pass their time in reading such books as the ship's library furnishes, in playing at whist or backgammon and walking about the decks. These, I am given to understand, are not the aristocracy of the States, who are the lawyers, physicians and landholders. They are, however, very favourable specimens of the shopocracy.

Our course up to this time has been slow in consequence of a continued and strong headwind, nearly from the West, which has also made the sea very rough and interrupted writing almost continually and reading very greatly. The stewards and waiters on board are civil and attentive, the fare good and the beds clean and sweet, and in a better state of body and mind I might be content or even be pleased with my situation. But in good [faith] it is far from so.

I had negotiated before coming on board and had proposed to the Captain that there should be daily prayers read by myself as chaplain in some part of the ship where they who liked might attend without interfering with others. He told me,

[8]John, 1st Earl Russell (1792–1878), Whig and Liberal politician who served twice as Prime Minister of the United Kingdom.
[9]Sir Charles Metcalfe, Governor General of Canada West, 1843-45.
[10]Thomas Salmon. *Modern History: or, The Present State of all Nations*, 3 vols. (London, 1744-46).

however, it was expressly forbidden in their orders and regulations and that on acct. of the various sects who were on board, for in case one minister should be allowed to hold forth in one part of the ship, another might claim a like privilege in another part, and as the Captain emphatically observed we should have two or three "holding forth" at the same time. I, of course, submitted to the orders and regulations. I found another very prevailing obstacle, viz., that for two or three days both I and Palairet were too poorly to have conducted the service, and very few indeed, perhaps hardly one, for the first day or two well enough to attend. However, there was no cabin or apartment sufficiently private, and in rough weather the creaking of the timbers and rolling of the vessel would have made it difficult whether to read or hear. I managed to read the Psalms and Lessons to myself daily.

Sunday, June 9

At half past ten o'clock there was service (*sicut est mos*)[11] in the saloon. The sailors who could be spared attended and most of the passengers. I and Palairet divided the service and I preached. All behaved well, and many used their prayer books (Americans and others). When there is no clergyman on board, the Captain reads the service and a sermon. Palairet read the Lessons, and on coming to the 29th verse of 10 St. Mark, the Second Lesson, he was so overpowered by his feelings as to be unable to proceed, and I took the book from him.[12] There was no afternoon service, but the evening was spent quietly and becomingly by all. It was a calm, beautiful evening: the horizon very wide, but my thoughts ranged wider, for I was in heart and spirit at Bicknor all the while my feet were pacing the narrow deck and my eyes gazing upon the blue waters before me. It was a solemn time. There were several gulls and Mother Carey's Chickens [storm petrels] following the wake of the ship. Would I have done so if I had enjoyed their liberty and ability! Yet may I not hope that I am like them heaven taught and heaven sent?

Monday, June 10

This morning disappointed the hopes and expectations which the calm, lovely evening of yesterday had inspired. It began to blow again before morning and during the day increased to a gale. Being right in our teeth, we made but slow progress. It continued to blow heavily the whole day and rained a good deal. Altogether, it was the most uncomfortable day we have had, and many who had recovered from the

[11]*Sicut est mos*: As is the habit.

[12]Mark 10 : 29-30: And Jesus answered and said, Verily I say unto you, There is no man that hath left house, or brethren, or sisters, or father, or mother, or wife, or children, or lands, for my sake, and the gospel's, but he shall receive an hundredfold now in this time, houses, and brethren, and sisters, and mothers, and children, and lands, with persecutions; and in the world to come eternal life.

seasickness became ill a second time. Happily, I was not of that number: but yet was unable to do more than read light books. I got through the 2nd vol. of Featherstonhaugh's *Excursions in America*.

Tuesday, June 11, St. Barnabas

Could not sleep at all during the last night, owing to the constant creaking of the timbers and tossing of the ship. The day was fine, but the wind still high and against us and the rolling of the ship greater than ever. I, however, managed to write up my diary to this point and look over my accts. : I read Burton's acct. of the religious communities in Australia. A very instructive but disheartening book.[13]

Wednesday, June 12

Perdidi diem literally[14] — for I made up my diary this day, as stated under the head of Tuesday, and fully thought we had not got farther than Tuesday. What, therefore, is said under that day of the weather applies to this day, Wednesday.

Thursday, June 13

The preceding night was fair and calm, and I had pleasant and refreshing sleep. The whole day was calm, and we made good progress. We saw a large brig standing towards England about noon. I took advantage of the calm to look over the papers &c in my despatch box and wrote up my accts. Nothing remarkable occurred during the day. All seemed in good humour with themselves and the fair weather.

Friday, June 14

This day we came into the fogs and cold of the Banks. The fog came on before noon, and the thermometer on deck sank to 42°. The sea, however, was quite calm, and the wind being for a time from the north-east, we put up canvass and made gallant way. In the evening, we saw an iceberg.

Saturday, June 15

This morning, after a calm and favourable night, though very foggy and cold, we came on the Banks of Newfoundland. There was considerable but not dense fog, widely extended and continuous. The cold was not so great as yesterday, and the

[13]Sir William Westbrooke Burton, *The State of Religion and Education in New South Wales* (London, 1840).

[14]*Diem perdidi*: "I have lost a day," expression attributed to the Emperor Titus characterizing a day in which he had done nothing for his subjects.

sun occasionally struggled through the fog. We saw a fishing vessel at anchor, occupied in its trade, and presuming it to be from Newfoundland I exclaimed, "I shall see thee again at Philippi."[15] The fog was by no means oppressive but on the contrary bracing and exhilarating. The sea still continued very calm and our motion proportionally smooth and rapid. I am well satisfied with this first taste of my diocese. Would to God there were nothing more chilling than its winds or more perplexing than its fog!

Sunday, June 16

The fog had cleared away, or rather had been left behind this morning, but it was still cold, the wind coming down from the north and northeast. We were making rapid progress, having all the sails spread.

At 10½ o'clock we had our service in the saloon, as last Sunday. The Methodist preacher, as might be expected, according to their fast and loose principles, did not attend. The greater number of passengers, indeed nearly all, did and behaved well. The day passed off quietly. The evening was very fine. There was a strange mixture in my thoughts and feelings of past, present and future — pleasant, indifferent and painful. I read some of Newman's sermons[16] and Venn's letters[17] — both instructive though in widely different ways. We made rapid progress all day, though in the evening the wind was less favourable. We saw several vessels, some timber vessels sailing to Quebec, others fishing.

The coast of Nova Scotia along which we passed the whole day, lying to the North, presents a low, undulating surface without any bold or striking features, of which our captain complained as getting no landmarks in times of hazard or doubt and equally complained of want of liberality in the people of Nova Scotia that they did not erect suitable and sufficient marks, which might be done at trifling expense and would be of great service. As we drew nearer to the land, we noticed the fir or pine of stunted growth in considerable numbers and clearings between and among them for cultivation, which presented a very green and refreshing appearance to eyes which had so long rested only on the wild and wasteful ocean. There are dangerous breakers near the shore and a picturesque little island called Devil's Island.[18]

[15]Feild refers to Shakespeare's *Julius Caesar*, 4.3: 283-84, wherein Brutus asks, "Then I shall see thee again?" The Ghost replies, "Ay, at Philippi"

[16]John Henry Newman, *Plain Sermons by Contributors to the "Tracts for the Times"* (London, 1834). John Henry Newman (1801-1890) was a priest in the Church of England received into the Roman Catholic Church in 1845. Earlier, he had been a major figure in the Oxford Movement.

[17]Henry Venn, *The Life and a Selection of Letters* (London, 1834).

[18]Devil's Island, situated at the mouth of Halifax harbour, consists of approximately 27 acres.

Passing these, we came about 5 o'clock to the entrance of the harbour, where on a projecting point stands a small, round lighthouse. We were then fairly in the harbour, and a more beautiful one it is hardly possible to desire or conceive. We had passed also an island called MacNab's Island to our right as we entered, well cultivated, the property of a private individual. When we entered, I saw on the one side more cottages and patches which reminded me of the Whitchurch settlements and cottages as seen from New [Wem] or still more of the St. Briavels settlement as seen from Llandogo.[19] Patches of ground cultivated and fenced with cottages at the bottom — only the hills were not so high and steep. On the other (north) side were the firs and patches of green land among them, but flat and comparatively unoccupied. The harbour itself reminded me both of Plymouth Sound and of the River Mersey. There is a beautiful island called George's Island, a little way in, which reminded me of Drake's Island at Plymouth but is now quite green — not rocky or lofty like Drake's Island. Upon this we found an encampment (about 20 white tents) of soldiers who on the way to Jamaica were wrecked (not at this spot) and are now detained till the heat of the summer is past. There is also a little round fort on the summit and some wooden buildings near the water. The little island is very green at this season of the year and the appearance altogether very lovely. On the north side of the harbour is a town or settlement named Dartmouth which strongly reminded me of Birkenhead and Woodside on the Cheshire side of the Mersey, while Halifax corresponded to Liverpool on the other side.

Halifax recedes slightly on a slope from the sea and presents a novel and picturesque appearance. The houses are chiefly of wood and covered with shingle, but being large and lofty they have an imposing appearance. The quays are wooden stages running into the harbour at regular intervals and distances; between these the vessels are drawn up waiting for freight. These vessels, which are only staying for a short time, as our steamer, draw up at the end of the stage or flake. The harbour is of sufficient size to hold all the navies of all Europe, and though not presenting the immense concourse of ships which we see in Plymouth Sound or the Mersey, there are enough to give signs of commercial life and wealth. I was struck by an Indian canoe of bark occupied by four Indians, two with paddles. Their dark hair and eyes and swarthy complexions and contemplative, almost melancholy looks were strange and striking. They seemed quite of another race, not only in blood but in mind and destiny.

Monday, June 17

After a good night in which good progress was made, the morning rose beautiful, clear and bright and much warmer than yesterday. The coast of Nova Scotia was distinguished to the north and soon after 9 o'clock some houses also. The Captain

[19]Llandogo: a village in Monmouthshire set on a steep hillside overlooking the River Wye, the Wye Valley and across into the Forest of Dean, Gloucestershire.

gives us good hopes of reaching Halifax by 6 o'clock. There being no wind from north there appears no danger of a fog on the coast, which at this season of the year is often a hindrance. We may hope, then, with God's blessing, to reach the land again this evening after little more than 13 days sail. And how wonderfully have we been preserved and blessed hitherto — over all this deep and wide ocean have we passed without accident or hindrance, nay with abundant comfort, ease and enjoyment. O! That men would therefore praise the Lord for his goodness and declare the wonders that he doeth for the children of men.[20]

We landed at Halifax at 6 o'clock by their time and found the Bishop of Nova Scotia [John Inglis][21] and his archdeacon [Robert Willis] waiting to receive me. There was a considerable crowd of persons on the shore, some anxious about friends in England, no doubt, some about O'Connell and the state of Ireland[22] and other matters of importance, but the first question I heard asked was, "Who was the winner of the Derby!" *O! Vanas hominum mentes!*[23] The answer I did not hear but perceived that it caused immense consternation and disgust in the anxious inquirer, who, I believe, was an officer named Allegue, a brother of one of our passengers. The Governor, Lord Falkland,[24] was on the quay among other spectators. The Master of the boat (Lieutenant Roberts) was taken ill just as we touched land and was unable to proceed on shore with his mail. The seizure seemed to be of an apoplectic nature. I went with the Bishop of Nova Scotia in his carriage to his residence and found there Mrs. Inglis and 3 daughters — agreeable persons and well favoured. Palairet stayed behind to look for the luggage. All mine was happily brought safe and sound to the hotel. One of his packages was missing. He came in to tea about nine o'clock. At ten o'clock, we had prayers and then departed safe and sound to our hotel. *Dieu merci* [Thank God].

On going to the Bishop's house we stopped for a moment at the Governor's house and saw Lord Falkland. I sent letters which I had written during the voyage to Mr. Bridge[25] by the Newfoundland packet ship, to Mrs. Pattrick, Miss Davies, G. Pattrick, Mr. Burdon, Ernest Hawkins, the Bishop of London.

[20]Psalm 107: 15: Oh that men would praise the Lord for his goodness, and for his wonderful works to the children of men!

[21]John Inglis (1777-1850) was the third bishop of Nova Scotia and the son of Bishop Charles Inglis.

[22]Daniel O'Connell (1775-1847), Irish political leader during the first half of the nineteenth century who championed Irish nationalism.

[23]*O! Vanas hominum mentes, O! Pectora cæca*. Latin proverb: "Oh, empty minds. Oh, dull hearts of men!"

[24]Lucius Bentinck Cary, 10th Viscount Falkland (1803–1884), British colonial administrator and Liberal politician, became Governor of Nova Scotia in 1840, after the recall of Sir Colin Campbell. He opposed the movement led by Joseph Howe for responsible government.

[25]Rev. Thomas F. Bridge (1807-1856), Vicar-General and Episcopal Commissary in Newfoundland.

I found letters waiting for me with the Bishop of Nova Scotia (1) from Mr. Bridge containing the account of Mr Cowan's serious illness[26] and the death of Mr. Blackman's[27] daughter; (2) from the Revd. Dr. [Richard] Tucker, Bishop's Commissary and Rural Dean in Bermuda, soliciting an appointment to the same offices and announcing the resignation of the living of Pagets and Warwick by the Rev. Mr. [S.P.] Musson, who has been presented to a living in Jamaica; (3) the form of resignation from the said Mr. Musson; and (4) an application from Dr. [James] Murray for an appointment to the said preferment. Came in the evening with Palairet to the Halifax Hotel, where I found a good sitting room with bedrooms adjoining prepared for us, which looked pleasantly upon the harbour.

Tuesday, June 18

After a beautiful sleep for and in which I needed not and missed not the rocking of the good packet ship, I found myself in a spacious apartment with only my good friend Palairet at breakfast. The change from the noisy saloon and vivacious Americans and bustling waiters was very agreeable. Just after breakfast, I was visited by Mr. Job of Newfoundland, on his way to Liverpool to obtain instructions for the establishment of gas works in St. John's — to be ready, as he said, to light the Cathedral![28] Soon after I was visited by the Bishop of Nova Scotia, by Archdeacon Willis, Mr. [William] Cogswell and others. I saw the *Caledonia* steam packet go past for Liverpool between 11 and 12 o'clock.

The morning was beautiful, and the island with its white tents was quite a picture. I never so wished to be able to draw. How I should like to send a sketch home. A fog came stealing from the sea about 10 o'clock with a south wind which increased during the day and very much hid the distant view but cooled the air, which otherwise might have been expected to be sultry. We took a walk with the Bishop, called on the Governor and dined with the Bishop.

The walk with the Bishop led us to the outskirts of the town through some fir groves which have been partly cleared with a view to cultivation. They are the property of a person who is trying to make them ornamental. There was a pretty shady walk through them leading down to the north arm of the sea which runs up a considerable distance between banks, which reminded me of the banks of the Dart. I tried to think the woods we went through like some of the enclosures in the neighbourhood of Bicknor. There were very few trees, except firs, which are small and stunted in growth. The bark very much resembles that of the oak at home. There were also a few maple, which is a valuable tree, a very few oak, ash and beech, but all very small size. There is also the white birch, the bark of which is used in covering ca-

[26]Rev. George B. Cowan, Harbour Grace, died in 1844.

[27]Rev. Charles Blackman, St. John's.

[28]The St. John's Gas Light Co. was incorporated in 1844 by an act of the Newfoundland legislature. One of those engaged in the enterprise was the merchant Robert Job.

noes, in platting, making strings, &c, and is or may be a substitute for paper. Near the town are some considerable commons, wild and rugged, though likely at some future time to be valuable if the town increases in size and wealth. Many houses are in course of erection about the town, chiefly of wood, though some are built of granite, some of brick, some of the slate stone of the immediate neighbourhood. Most of the houses have foundations of stone and brick. The lime comes from St. John, N.B., and some (as ballast) from Ireland. Wooden houses are still generally preferred, as dryer and warmer in winter. When built with care, they are expensive, but generally speaking the cost of a wooden house is not much more than half that of a similar building of stone.

The town of Halifax seems to consist of 4 or 5 long parallel streets running N and S and parallel also to the harbour. These rise one above the other and are wide and airy. They are crossed at right angles by short streets of communication which are also tolerably wide and roomy. In front of the houses is generally a wooden fence, which looks mean enough. The streets and roads are very dusty. Tar is in course of introduction, but only, I believe, for the use of porch-houses and [prisons]. The churches St. Paul's and St. George's and a chapel of ease to the latter are all of wood. St. Paul's has been built upwards of 80 years and is still in good repair. It is of such style as may be supposed.[29] Another chapel of ease is in contemplation in St. Paul's parish.

The fog here seems to be a very merciful provision, at least in summer, as it steals in from the sea with the south wind when otherwise we should say κᾳυσων εςᾶι and cools the air.[30] It is not thick or suffocating like a London fog, or even like a fog from the sea at Torquay. It spreads a veil, continually varying in density, and shifted by the winds over the town and harbour and the banks but does not extend far into the country. It is occasionally so dense as to prevent vessels coming into the harbour, even a whole day, and it frequently hides the land more or less from the view of those entering into the harbour.

Local difficulties are made about the constitution of the Church, the subscribers wishing in some instances to have the appointment of the clergyman and other privileges, and requiring it seems to be coaxed by the Bishop. As it is, subscribers of £100 are to have first choice of pew, subscribers of £50 second choice, and so on in proportion — 300 sittings it is hoped will be reserved for the poor as free.

The fog is, I think, refreshing; at least I felt no fatigue after a long walk, which was very encouraging and comfortable. About 7 o'clock it came on to rain heavily,

[29]Founded by proclamation of George II in 1749, the building was erected in the summer of 1750 and opened its doors in September. The architectural style was based on that of St. Peter's Church, Vere Street, London, designed by James Gibbs, a follower of Sir Christopher Wren.

[30]The Greek phrase κᾳυσων εςᾶι can be transliterated as *kausōn estai* and loosely translated as "it's going to be hot". The same verb turns up in 2 Peter 3:10 and 3:12, as well as Luke 12: 55.

the wind having got to the east, from which quarter rain is generally expected. We had a pleasant party at the Bishop's consisting of his Lordship, Mrs. Inglis, 3 misses Inglis, Archdeacon Willis, Revd. Cogswell, the Chaplain, Dr. [Thomas] Twining, Revd. [Robert] Uniacke, Major and Mrs. Tryon (the last a daughter of Sir John Harvey),[31] Palairet and [Edward] Newfoundland. Two of the ladies played on the piano, to Palairet's content.

Wednesday, June 19

I dreamt last night that I was again a boy at Rugby! and, as a not unusual frolic, had taken possession of my friend Currie's bed, intending by force of arms, bolster and shoes, to keep him out. After waiting in expectation some time, I saw him approach and I cried out, "I am come to teach you the evils of irresponsible government." He stooped down, as he was wont, to give me one of his dear, fond kisses, and the sweet vision vanished. I awoke in the Halifax Hotel, Nova Scotia, and he, dear fellow, is probably taking his siesta in Calcutta. May his dreams be equally pleasant — and when he awakes may his eyes rest upon real, pleasant objects of his care and affection. Though I shall never again kiss him, I can love him and pray for him and can rejoice in the thought that he loves and prays for me, notwithstanding his many objects of nearer and dearer concern and attachment.

The morning broke with a slight fog, which cools the air nicely. I breakfasted at 8½ o'clock with Palairet and just after breakfast received an invitation to dine with Archdeacon Willis tomorrow at 7 o'clock. Went to St. Paul's Church at 11 o'clock — morning prayers with the Litany, read by Mr. Cogswell, the Archdeacon's curate. At two o'clock, the Bishop drove out myself and Palairet to the point at the north commanding a view of the North Arm. Afterwards, the Bishop, Mrs. and Miss Inglis took me in the Bishop's carriage along a beautiful road coasting the Bedford Basin to a place called the Lodge, formerly a residence of the late Duke of Kent,[32] now in ruins. It was a handsome house with a suitable library, large stables, [paved] as in the grounds &c., all now fallen into decay. The grounds are now the property of Lord Wilton.[33] The drive along the basin and the basin itself are exceedingly pretty. A great deal of pine, white and brown birch, a few beech and hemlock trees. These latter resemble the common garden cedars, and their bark is used in tanning. We visited in our drive the chapel of ease to St. George's just built by Mr.

[31]Sir John Harvey (1778-1852), British army officer, Lieutenant-Governor of Prince Edward Island, 1836-37; New Brunswick, 1837-41; Newfoundland, 1841-46; and Nova Scotia, 1846-52.

[32]Prince Edward Augustus, Duke of Kent and Strathearn (1767-1820), fourth son of George III and father of Queen Victoria. In 1799, he was appointed commander-in-chief of British forces in North America and for most of his tenure lived in Halifax, where he was instrumental in shaping the port's defences.

[33]Arthur Edward Holland Grey Egerton (1833-1885), 3rd Earl of Wilton.

Uniacke about 3 miles from the town, not yet consecrated. On our return, we drove through the Dockyards, which are quiet and very clean and capable of being turned to acct. Dined at 7 with the Bishop of Nova Scotia.

It is very curious to see the lilacs and honeysuckles now in full and fresh blossom, which had faded away a month ago in England. There appear to be very few other flowering trees. The acacia is now just putting out its first leaves — and they appear thin, pale and frightened. All the leaves seem very deficient in substance and colour as compared with the trees in England, indicating a short and sickly existence. The same is the appearance in the kitchen gardens, with respect at least to the date and progress of vegetation. Peas are a few inches above ground, onions just weeded for the first time, currants hardly formed and other like appearances: all, however, are properly attended to, seem healthy. The gardens are generally very mean — no gravel, few flowers, many weeds. The borders of boards, broken or thrown down, and the walls also of boards against which are commonly trained currants. Cucumbers and salads there are — but celery and asparagus seem rare. The Bishop's garden is neat and the nicest I have seen.

N.B. The above was written before I had seen Col. Bazalgette's[34] garden, where is a small conservatory with a few grapes, or at least vine trees which may possibly, though not probably, ripen some fruit. There are also 3 peach trees with better promise & one apricot. The kitchen and flower garden are superior to the Bishop's and more forward.

I saw this day in the streets a squaw, i.e., an Indian married woman, and on the east side of the Bedford Basin several of their wigwams, which very much resemble the little huts which the wood colliers make to put in their tools &c in the woods. There are many Negroes always to be seen in the streets. They were from a colony of Negroes planted in this neighbourhood during the American war; having been taken from the Americans, they are called the Chesapeake Negroes.

Thursday, June 20

At half past ten o'clock was taken by the Bishop of Nova Scotia with Palairet to see the fort, where considerable fortifications are yet in progress under the superintendence of Col. Calder. The 52nd Regiment and the Rifle Brigade are now in barracks near the fort. The works are very interesting, exhibiting amazing thought and contrivance, especially in a covered way which goes all round the outside of the fortifications, from which on one side are communications with mines towards the town &c and on the other side openings to the ditch which surrounds the fort. From thence, we went to the near cemetery, now ready for consecration. Part is intended for the members of the Church and will be consecrated; part is for the Dissenters.

[34]Col. John Bazalgette (1784-1868), an army officer involved in the affairs of Nova Scotia for forty-three years.

The Roman Catholics have another to and for themselves at a distance. Lunched at the Bishop's.

At two o'clock went over to George's Island under the escort of Col. Bazalgette. Several ladies (Mrs. and Miss Inglis and others) accompanied us in the boat. The view from the island upon the town and harbour exceedingly pleasing & leaving a great expanse of water on either side, and the towns of Halifax and Dartmouth sloping down to the water and the waves kissing them. The island itself is small, containing [a] covered fort with many guns. This is intended to command and protect the entrance into the harbour. In tents (about 30) the Royals are encamped who were shipwrecked in the Gulf of St. Lawrence. We were treated first with instrumental and then with vocal music by the band. They are taught to sing by Lieut. Whitmore, a brother, as I found, of my friends Charles and Ainslie Whitmore. He gives much attention to their instruction, and the result is very satisfactory. While at Quebec, they took the church music (chanting and canticles &c) upon themselves, to the great gratification of the Bishop and congregation. The Commanding Officer is Col. Hill. All the officers speak in warm praises of the good effect produced by the vocal pursuits and performances upon the manners of the soldiers. The officers had prepared a lunch in their mess room. We returned in the boats at 5 o'clock. At 7 o'clock went to dine with Archdeacon Willis, who has daughters, and several clergy and Dr. Henry.[35]

The master and mistress of the National Schools (man and wife) receive £150 a year with a house and fuel, and their daughter, unmarried and living with them, receives besides £25 for attending to the sale of the books of the S.P.C.K. depot.[36] This is a very ample supply of bibles, prayer books and tracts and well arranged for sale.

The Bishop of N.S. was evidently consternified [*sic*] at my refusing to dine out on Friday. Indeed, to decline an invitation or neglect to return a call seems nothing less than high treason, and in the case of the Governor something a great deal worse.

Friday, June 21

Went with the Bishop of Nova Scotia to the prayers at St. Paul's Church. After service went to the National School, where were about 87 boys and upwards of 100 girls. The boys are well taught and well disciplined, the Dissenters not required to learn the Ch. Catechism. Out of 126 girls the mistress said there were but 22 members of our Communion. Almost all had long plaited tails and looked bold enough. The Dissenters are allowed to go to their own schools and chapels on Sunday. We

[35]Dr. Walter Henry (1791-1860), Staff Surgeon in the British Army. See his *Events of a Military Life: Being Recollections After Service in the Peninsular War, Invasion of France, the East Indies, St. Helena, Canada, and Elsewhere*, 2 vols. (London: W. Pickering, 1843).

[36]The Society for Promoting Christian Knowledge is the oldest Anglican mission society, founded in 1698 by Thomas Bray and a group of friends. It is now most widely known for publishing Christian books.

then went to the African School, where the children of our Negroes are educated, boys and girls together, of various ages from 3 to 12 years. Master and mistress inefficient. Some of the children seem clever and have sweet voices but are very imperfectly taught.

Went to see the Public Offices and House of Assembly — goodly buildings enough but very dirty. The Commons are called the Assembly, presided over by a Speaker, and the Upper House is the Council, presided over by the Governor. The Bishop has a seat on the Council, and prayers are read every day by the Archdeacon, their chaplain. Made calls and spent evening at the hotel.

Saturday, June 22

The fog this morning turned into rain, or rather fog and rain came together and continued all day. I did not leave the hotel during the morning. Finished a letter to Cardin and received a visit from Col. Bell, who is in command of the Royals. Dined at 7 o'clock at the Bishop's house and met various colonels and majors, a Mr. Jeffrey and Mr. Cunard.[37] Went to dinner and returned in Col. Bazalgette's carriage. Rain all day.

Sunday, June 23

Went to St. Paul's Sunday Schools at 10 o'clock with the Bishop. Boys and girls together in the same room but in separate classes, instructed by young ladies (the Archdeacon's daughters &c.), shopkeepers and others as in some towns of England. The Curate, Mr. Cogswell, attends and directs. The attendance is voluntary and very irregular. The chief object seems to be to carry them through some portions of the Bible, by which means one of the teachers informed me they gave the children a complete system of Divinity!! What is wanting in the Scriptures is made up from hymn books and catechisms from the Sunday School Union and other equally "authentic" sources.[38] The girls were free and forward in their manners and paid little attention to their teachers. The classes consisted in several cases of not more than 3 or 4 children, and nothing like discipline was enforced. All this is said to be due to the number of Dissenting congregations and schools, but perhaps the number of these may be ascribed to the want of discipline in the Church.

Went to St. Paul's Church at 11 o'clock. On my asking the Archdeacon whether I should give notice of holy days and fasting days to be observed in the week, he answered, "There are none this week." And on my saying in reply there were two, St.

[37]Sir Samuel Cunard (1787-1865), Canadian-born shipping magnate who founded the Cunard Line.

[38]The American Sunday School Union was founded in 1824 in Philadelphia to promote Sunday schools and their ideals of early literacy and spiritual development in children. It was also a significant publisher and a provider of books and periodicals for children.

John Baptist on Monday, St. Peter the Apostle on Saturday, he said, "Yes, but we only give notice of them when they fall on Wednesday and Friday." A large congregation at St. Paul's, but of the same free and easy ways as the children of the schools, scarcely any kneeling. The psalms and canticles were well chanted by the singers of the Royals, led by Lieut. Whitmore — I preached. In the afternoon, I went to the Sunday Schools of St. George's Parish, of which Mr. Uniacke is the incumbent. These are conducted in nearly the same manner as St. Paul's, but the classes were fuller and better attended and the children more subdued in their appearance and respectful in their deportment. The teachers seemed equally well satisfied of the ability and knowledge, and there was the same strange admixture of heretical books with the Holy Scriptures.

Almost every other girl was armed with a parasol, and of course curls and tails in proportion. I preached at St. George's, a round church with 3 tiers of galleries, just like a theatre — the singers behind the pulpit and over the altar. N.B. The altar at St. Paul's is at the north end and in St. George's at the west! The height of the pulpit is quite alarming.

Dined with the Bishop and his family at 5 o'clock and at 7 went again to St. Paul's, where was evening service. The sermon by a Revd. Jonathan Short, a clergyman from the Diocese of Toronto. I was very much struck by the appearance of the poor Blacks in the open benches of the middle passage. None others would sit near them. One old man seemed very attentive and devout. The women were generally in light straw bonnets with white ribbons and stuffing. This, with the large whites of the eyes, set off their black faces to advantage.

Monday, June 24, St. John Baptist

Woke with a splitting headache. A beautiful bright morning. Heard the deep bell of the Roman Catholic chapel at 7 o'clock but no summons from either of the churches. A temperance party (Roman Catholics) went with a band of music on one of the steamers for a picnic up the harbour at 10 o'clock, many labourers, who take their holiday freely. Mr. Cogswell called at 10 o'clock. I went with him to see a small yacht of 40 tons, old measure, or 28 new, in which he had been out 3 days and nights and very comfortably lodged and entertained. Went to give directions about my episcopal seal. The Bishop called at 12 o'clock and Mr. Uniacke at 2 o'clock.

Dined with the Governor and Lady Falkland at Government House. Lady Falkland was one of the Fitzclarences, an accomplished lady, paints and plays very well. Lord Falkland is a bluff, well meaning man, came out under the Whigs and professes himself so but does not conceal his dislike of the popular party here. Thinks it impossible for any high-minded person to deal with them and is anxious to be relieved — and says that no friend of his shall come into his place. Describes his predicament as like that of a man walking through a bog where reptiles continually crawl and cling about his legs. Having such sentiments and expressing them, he is not, of course, popular. He, at the commencement of his government, alienated the Conservatives, and now he finds the Radicals turn against him. Among other measures unpalatable to him, they have reduced his salary from £3,500 to £2,500. There were about 14 people at dinner, everything very handsome and good on the table. The house itself and furniture is somewhat dingy. They have one child only, a son, for whose benefit Mr. Torre is engaged as tutor and lives in the house. Mr. Torre is of university and knows Carden. The Bishop of N.S. did not dine there but sent his carriage, notwithstanding, both to take and bring us back.

Tuesday, June 25

Three weeks have passed the day since we embarked at Liverpool. It is hard to realize the change that has come over our place and prospects. They tell us we are now in Halifax of Nova Scotia, in North America, on the western side of the great Atlantic, 2,500 miles from old England. They tell us that a few years ago Indians and heathens inhabited these shores, dwelling in wigwams and moving about in little bark canoes. Now we see Englishmen and Christians, churches, colleges, schools, Houses of Assembly and courts of judicature; we see streets and shops thronged with busy, intelligent folk, talking our native language, wearing the same clothes, apparently engaged in the same pursuits, and certainly shewing the same friendliness and hospitality. We see a magnificent harbour frequented, almost crowded, with gallant ships, among which many, most, are bearing aloft the [. . .] flag of England, the flag which has braved a thousand years the battle and the breeze. It is possible, then, that this is America — not England?

Walked out with the Bishop of N.S. and two of his amiable daughters to visit the penitentiary, which is beautifully situated near the North Arm (as it is called), an arm of the sea very much resembling in its shape and the shape of its banks the wide parts of the River Dart. Took a very pleasant walk through the fir woods and saw many wild flowers and fruits — strawberry, bogberry, and dewberry — the last much resembling the whisenberry of the Forest of Dean — azalea, calurias, and rhododendrons also grow wild but are not fine. The scent from the fir or spruce is very pleasing. The strawberries are abundant and good and regularly sold in the markets; very few are grown in the gardens.

At 7 o'clock we dined at Major Tryon's with the Bishop and Mrs. Inglis and met Sir Charles and Lady Adam,[39] the Archdeacon and Lieut. Cayton, R.N.

Wednesday, June 26

Started at 10 o'clock by stagecoach for Windsor with the Bishop. A fine morning. The distance from Halifax to Windsor is 45 miles. The road is a pretty good one.

[39]Admiral Sir Charles Adam (1780-1853), Commander-in-Chief of the North America and West Indies Station.

Has been formed nearly 50 years. It runs along the side of the harbour and Bedford Basin to the head of the basin, the whole of which is exceedingly fair and pleasant on a fine day. On the left hand, or west side, lies the Duke of Kent's folly, the house which he built and park which he made — the former fallen down and the latter much dirt and devastation. After passing the head of this lake or basin, we passed between uncleared woods of pine and fir on either side, looking grim and ghastly enough but presenting now and then openings of great beauty: that is, where there was an extensive view over the woods, and an admixture of deciduous trees with the everlasting fir made the scene of a more English character.

The clearings are ugly and uninteresting, presenting a few acres, perhaps a farm of wretchedly cultivated land with the widest possible wooden fence. The fences are of two kinds: one is called the worm fence and consists of long fir poles from 12 to 14 ft. placed one upon another to the number of 5, 6 or 7 and crossed by others at an angle of about 45° with two slight poles supporting them and resting against them at the place of crossing. The other is called a pitch-pole fence and consists of poles lying aslant in a straight line and supported by upright poles. In the latter case, the upright poles are generally tied to the aslant ones, but the former there is no fastening band of any kind.

The country among the woods is very cold and stony till we arrive at the summit of a ridge of hills about . . . miles from Halifax. On descending these hills towards Windsor we lose the effect of the sea air entirely, and the climate is perceptibly warmer. The soil improves, the trees are more luxuriant, the grass more rich and green, and the scene more varied. Some beautiful distant views reminded me of Holden, near Exeter. As we got nearer to Windsor, we got upon land reclaimed from the sea by dikes, or rather salt marshes converted into pasture lands by keeping out the flowing tides. These were brought into cultivation by the Acadians and are now very rich and productive. Many of the meadows, it is said, produce 3 tons of hay to the acre, and the oat crops are equally abundant.

The first place of stopping is called Sackville, near which is the Sackville River, and Sackville Church nicely placed on a hill. This place is 14 miles from Halifax, and to this we came with 6 horses (3 pairs) driven in hand by one coachman, who seemed to have them as much in command as our coachman. The horses are not large and handsome but very respectable and shew some blood, though not well trained. We saw several lakes among the trees, which are pretty as a variety in the landscape. We reached Windsor without accident about 5 o'clock. Two old-fashioned maiden ladies of Halifax were our companions the first stage.

Windsor is a very pretty village at this time of the year — clean and airy — with well-built houses of wood, many new, and productive gardens — apples, pears and plums being the staple fruits. A good deal of cider is made in the neighbourhood. The Windsor River, an arm of the sea, comes up to the village and brings in a steamer.

There is also some little traffic with the United States, chiefly in gypsum or plaster, which abounds in this neighbourhood. There is a very good village inn kept by a man named Brass, formerly a servant in Lord Francis Egerton's family,[40] and in his sitting room I found to my surprise Landreth's best engraving[41] with pictures of Sir Robert Peel, Lord Francis Egerton, Bootle-Wilbraham[42] &c so that we seemed quite at home. We dined at 6 o'clock and after dinner strolled about the village and the grounds of Judge Haliburton, the renowned Sam Slick,[43] accompanied by the Rector of the parish, Mr. [Edwin] Gilpin. We saw also the fort where the poor Acadians were entrapped and deprived of their liberty before their removal from the country. This fort affords a pretty panorama. The natural beauties of the place were less acceptable and attractive when we learned that the people are divided and distracted by every kind of dissent.

Thursday, June 27

At ten o'clock this morning we proceeded, attended by Mr. Stevenson, the mathematical professor at the College, to visit the University of Nova Scotia, called and known by the name of King's College, Windsor.[44] The first foundation, object and rules of the College are detailed in the statutes and charter. The buildings are a long, narrow range or row of wood with five doors approached by flights of 5 or 6 steps, all of wood. At the left hand end is the President's house, whose name is McCawley.[45] He is a married man, and his wife and daughter live in this house with him. One of the other entrances leads to the refectory, a hall which is also the lecture room. Over the refectory is the library, in which are about 6 sets of double shelves standing at right angles to the sidewalks between the windows, as in [the] library at Queen's College [Oxford]. There are many valuable books, chiefly presents from England. There are also philosophical apparatus of various kinds, as telescopes,

[40]Francis Egerton, 1st Earl of Ellesmere (1800-1857).

[41]Wood engravings from the seed catalogue of David Landreth and Sons.

[42]Edward Bootle-Wilbraham (1771-1853), 1st Baron Skelmersdale, British politician.

[43]Thomas Chandler Haliburton (1796-1865), born in Windsor, studied at King's College and was called to the bar in 1820. Named a judge of the Inferior Court of Common Pleas in 1829, he was elevated twelve years later to the Supreme Court of Nova Scotia. Haliburton began his writing career as a historian, but in the 1830s he turned to humorous and satirical fiction to express his Tory opinions on political and social questions. In 1835, he contributed to Joseph Howe's journal *The Novascotian* a series of satirical sketches entitled "Recollections of Nova Scotia." Their popularity led him to expand them into *The Clockmaker; or, The Sayings and Doings of Samuel Slick, of Slickville* (1836).

[44]The University of King's College, Canada's oldest chartered university, was founded in 1789 in Windsor by a group of United Empire Loyalists led by Bishop Charles Inglis, the first Anglican bishop of Nova Scotia. The statutes were modeled on those of Oxford and placed under the patronage of the Archbishop of Canterbury.

[45]Rev. Dr. George McCawley, President from 1836 to 1875.

compasses, electrical instruments, theodolites &c, &c. The young men may have books upon application to the President but are not otherwise admitted to the library. There is a small chapel lately made out of a set of rooms, to which there is a private entrance from the President's house and another for the students. The other entrances lead to students' rooms. The students have each a sitting room bedroom and have a lumber [i.e., storage] room, and a set of rooms extends through the thickness or depth of the house. These are commodious enough but generally with the staircases dirty and in bad repair.

The building is quite flat at the top, so that nothing more plain and unpretending in appearance could be well conceived. There are about 70 acres of land adjoining the College which are occupied by the President, Professor and Steward for their own use and profit. The number of students in residence last term was 22. There is no means of confining them at night, which might be the reason of serious evils. The present officers of the College are the President, Dr. McCawley, the mathematical professor, Rev. Mr. Stevenson, both educated at the College, and a steward who provides for the table &c. The President and Professor give all the instruction and regulate the discipline, and of course fill all other offices.

I saw some of the exercises (verse) performed by the students, some Greek, some Latin and some Spanish. They had several faults of syntax and prosody, which seemed to shew the teachers to be not very accurate scholars. Some of the students have made considerable progress in mathematics, reading the *Principia*,[46] the Differential Calculus,[47] Bland's *Hydrostatics*[48] &c. There is also a professor of modern languages, a Dr. Mantovani, who does not reside in the College buildings, though rooms are provided for him. Mr. Stevenson, the Professor, who is unmarried, does reside. The President and Professor seem to be earnest and careful according to their knowledge and opportunities. They examine also for the degrees and conduct all the affairs of the University under the direction of the Governors.

The students go to chapel twice in the day, at 6 o'clock in the morning and 4 in the afternoon. They dine at 5 o'clock. They breakfast and tea separately in their own rooms and dine in hall. In the morning they attend lectures &c. They have 4 years of 4 terms, as in Oxford, before they can take a B.A. degree and must reside 12 terms. There are 4 vacations — 2 of 2 months each at midsummer and Christmas and two

[46]*Philosophiæ Naturalis Principia Mathematica* (1687), a three-volume work by Isaac Newton containing the statement of Newton's laws of motion that formed the foundation of classical mechanics, as well as his law of universal gravitation and a derivation of Kepler's laws for the motion of the planets.

[47]The modern development of calculus is usually credited to Isaac Newton and Gottfried Leibniz, who provided independent and unified approaches to differentiation and derivatives. The key insight was the fundamental theorem of calculus relating differentiation and integration, rendering obsolete most previous methods for computing areas and volumes, not significantly extended since the time of Archimedes.

[48]Miles Bland, *The Elements of Hydrostatics* (Cambridge, 1824).

of a fortnight each at Easter and Whitsuntide. Any may reside during the short vacation but are under no discipline.

20,000 acres have been set apart in different parts of the province for the support of the College, which at present yield no return.

Dissenters are admitted and may take degrees in Arts and may be excused from attending chapel. One of the fruits of such a system I met with in a Mr. Crawley, a Baptist minister who had been regularly educated at the College and had seceded from the Church. Connected with the College is a school or academy.[49] The building is about 300 or 400 yards from the College — is chiefly intended for boarders but receives day scholars. At present, there are not more than 18 boarders — the numbers having much decreased of late — the master [Rev. William King] is a clergyman educated at the College, son of a former rector of the parish named King. I should suppose he is either inefficient or careless. He is married, and his wife does not seem to promote the interests of such an establishment. The same licence is allowed to the Dissenters here with respect to attendance at prayers as at the College. The buildings are good.

After visiting the College and School, we went to see the parish church and parsonage, accompanied by Mr. Gilpin, the Rector, who is an amiable, sensible man, anxious to improve the arrangements of his church. The Bishop then drove me about to see the neighbourhood and, among other places, to the farm of a Major King, who is a character. He has made a farm and ruined himself. We dined at the farm, having added Mr. Gilpin to our party.

Friday, June 28

Sam Slick was expected to call and would have done so, but was not shaven. Captain Denison, the brother of the Bishop of Salisbury, arrived at our little inn, returning from a fishing expedition. He was with a companion in a waggon brought from Halifax, to which place they proceeded on this day. We started in the coach with the Baptist minister, Mr. Crawley, and his family of his wife, 2 children, 3 nephews, 2 nieces and maid. We were 7 inside, some outside and the rest in a waggon!

We returned by the same road we had travelled on Wednesday and reached Halifax a little before 6 o'clock. Walked to see the Newfoundland steamer which had arrived this morning, having been detained a whole day at Arichat [Cape Breton Island] by contrary winds.[50] Drank tea in the hotel and wrote 10 pages of journal.

[49]King's Collegiate School, the oldest independent school in the Commonwealth outside the United Kingdom, traces its origins to 1788, when it was founded by Loyalists.

[50]Arichat: one of the oldest communities in Nova Scotia. In 1713, a permanent settlement was established, beginning the rapid economic rise of Isle Madame, where it is located.

Saturday, June 29, St. Peter's Day

At 7 o'clock heard the bell of the Roman Catholic chapel tolling, and the same was repeated three times during the day, but no sound from the Church, no note of prayer or praise in the Church. Such honour have God's saints in our church! Received letters from Mr. Bridge and the Governor of Bermuda — replied to the latter. Sealed up letters also to Mr. Polson, Ernest Hawkins, L. Carden, Dr. Feild, Dr. Tucker and Dr. Murray. Took berths in the steam packet for Newfoundland, lunched and dined with the Bishop of Nova Scotia. Met Captain Carden of the 52nd, a cousin of Lionel's, Captain Bradford of the Rifle Brigade, the Archdeacon and Capt. and Mrs. Tryon.

Sunday, June 30

Went across the harbour to Dartmouth. Too late for the packet by one minute, which hindered us 40 minutes, and we did not reach the church till half past eleven. Decent church and congregation but neither large. A Mr. [George] Morris the Rector. Palairet read prayers. I preached. Dreadfully silent congregation.

In the afternoon, I preached at St. Paul's Halifax. Dined with the Bishop. Palairet preached in the evening (3d service) at St. Paul's — preached very well, though with too many breaks and pauses. Read a good deal too slow in the morning.

In the evening, after the service, returned to drink tea at the Bishop's, who read a sermon.

Monday, July 1

Julia's birthday and Mrs. Wray's girls. Our last move to be made today. The steamer from England, announced at 9 o'clock in sight, reached the wharf at 12 o'clock, a fine morning; brought me a letter from Hawkins containing several others.

At 2 o'clock went to dine with the Bishop for the last time. Took leave of his kind, amiable family at 3½ o'clock, deeply touched and obliged by their hospitality. Nothing could exceed it, and as far as I could judge they are, all and each, as really amiable as hospitable. The Bishop drove us in his carriage to take leave of Mrs. Tryon (the daughter of Sir John and Lady Harvey) and thence to the wharf from which the Newfoundland steamer the *North America* was to start. Found her ready and waiting for us. Met on the wharf, besides the good Bishop, who attended us, the Archdeacon, Revd. Mr. Cogswell, Torro and Uniacke, Major Tryon and others. Embarked and left all pleasure behind us at ¼ past four o'clock. Found Mr. Crawley, the Baptist preacher, and his family on board. We had scarcely left the beautiful harbour of Halifax before fog and rain came on, and a cold, disagreeable evening ensued. So ended the pleasant episode of Halifax.

I posted letters this day: (1) the Governor of Bermuda, (2) Revd. Dr. Tucker, (3) Rev. Dr. Murray, (4) E. Hawkins, (5) Dr. Feild, (6) Lord Carden, (7) R. Davies, (8) Mr. Scott, (9) S. Burden, (10) C. Wray, (11) Mrs. Polson.

2. Halifax to St. John's

Visits to Portugal Cove, Torbay, Petty Harbour, Harbour Grace, Carbonear, Island Cove, Bishop's Cove, Spaniard's Bay, Bay Roberts, Bareneed, Port de Grave, Salmon Cove and Brigus

Tuesday, July 2

The morning broke, or rather did not break, through a thick fog which hindered us full 3 hours. We contrived, however, to creep into Arichat about 1 o'clock. On nearing the land, the fog dissipated as we left it behind, and we discovered a pretty harbour with several bays and islands. The land low — and apparently barren — but at this season looking green. This is one of the old French settlements, replenished by emigrants from Jersey and lately by Scotch. The inhabitants very generally talk French or Jersey French and are Romanists. The Roman Catholic chapel is large and lofty, I should guess 100 feet by 60. The seats on the floor all open and low, a large space concluded by the rails around the altar. The altar itself is handsome, was made at Quebec. Two nice paintings from Italy. A chest of drawers within the rails containing the priest's robes. Several surplices hanging up for acolytes &c. On the whole, the appearance was imposing and pleasing. The priest is a Frenchman and on good terms with the Protestant clergyman — too much so, it is said, to please his congregation.

The Protestant church is wretched in comparison, fitted up with confined pews and a pulpit in the centre at the east end, in front of which stands a Communion table. The clergyman is named Shaw. An old gentleman, Mr. Jane, dressed in his Sunday clothes, kindly came to meet me. He informed me [he] had resided 40 years there and his appearance are signs of his being some time out of humanity's or of fashion's reach. He is a collector of customs and a chief man of the island. Our Baptist friends left us here. We re-embarked about three o'clock and were soon enveloped in dense fog.

The passage money is £4 Sterling.

There is a captain on board who dines with the passengers (he is a Roman Catholic), two stewards, a waiter and a stewardess — the ladies' cabin is tolerably comfortable, much better at least than that of the gentlemen. Our berths open into our cabin or saloon, and there is one common washing place for passengers of all sorts, which is dark and dirty. Part of the crew also take their meals at the lower end of our cabin, and all the washing up is transacted there — but most gladly and thankfully would I abide in it with all its discomforts another fortnight to have some little comparative leisure and independence.

The passengers were a Baptist minister and his wife, child, 3 nephews and 2 nieces who left us at Arichat; a Dr. Henry, a medical man from Halifax going to inspect the state of the troops at St. John's; a Mr. Rendle of St. John's; young Mr. Blackman of St. John's, returning from Windsor; a lovely lass returning from Windsor to Arichat; and a Mr. Witherspoon, half English, half [...].

Thursday, July 4

This morning my eyes opened on the shores of Newfoundland. What a prospectus! Fog and clouds were hanging about it like a veil, and it seemed unwilling to shew its face. And what a face — an iron mask. Low slate rocks just high and steep enough to forbid access presented themselves for many miles, truly an ironbound coast. We neared the shore first at Cape Race about 7 o'clock in the morning and then coasted the whole way to St. John's. About 10 o'clock we came opposite to a settlement called Renews, where appeared several cottages and some attempts at cultivation and many fishing boats in front. Some curious rocks called the Butterpots running a considerable length along the island, parallel to the shore, formed the background, and altogether the scene was pretty and picturesque. Several small icebergs were against the shore.

In proceeding, we passed several small settlements and harbours, Ferryland, the Bay of Bulls, Petty Harbour &c. At each of these, we saw cottages on land and in harbour fishing boats busily employed. At the same named place we saw full 60 boats so at work with their red sails flapping in the wind and evidently doing execution. The coast presents the same barren, forbidding appearance the whole distance from Cape Race to St. John's, about 60 miles. We came in sight of St. John's, or rather of the Narrows, about 3 o'clock and reached the entrance of the harbour a little before 4 o'clock.

The entrance is striking and picturesque, reminding me in some particulars of the River Dart. There is not the same beautiful turn, but the rocks on either side are lofty and evidently torn asunder by some mighty convulsion and longing to meet again. On the north and right hand side, as we entered, a signal station crowns the hill, which is very steep. On the south side, the hill is more easy of ascent, sloping gently towards the water and not so lofty as its opposite neighbour. Both hills are clothed with a low brushwood not much larger or higher than gooseberry bushes and uniform as to present the appearance of a Negro's curly pate. On making the entrance, a long, narrow harbour lies before you which looks diminutive after Halifax harbour but is really commodious and safe. On either side of the harbour, but chiefly on the north, lies the town of St. John's.

We entered hastily, and my mind was so distracted that I could hardly form an opinion of the town itself. I saw, however, it was much meaner in its streets and buildings than Halifax. My eye was caught by the scaffold poles of an immense church which I easily guessed to be the Roman Catholic cathedral.[1] It is set on a hill at the back or west end of the town and is a very conspicuous and commanding object. I could have wished it devoted to a purer and more primitive form of worship. On the north side I saw the large stony Government House, also on a hill on the north side of the town and near it the picturesque little wooden church [St. Thomas's] built by Archdeacon [Edward] Wix. I was not permitted to continue my observations, for three boats were seen approaching the steamer, each intended for my accommodation or to do me honour. One was sent by the Governor (Sir John Harvey) and was directed by his eldest son. The 2nd was manned by the 2 clergy of the town with their churchwardens and the third by Capt. Elliot of HMS *Eurydice*, whose ship was lying in the harbour. Mr. [Thomas] Bridge and Mr. [Charles] Blackman, two clergymen, came on board the steamer and, having welcomed me to my diocese, directed me and assisted me into the Governor's boat, into which they also entered. The churchwardens in their boat addressed and welcomed me.

In 2 or 3 minutes, we were at the Queen's Wharf, where I found the soldiers of the Royal Newfoundland Companies[2] drawn up in number, I should suppose 60 or 70, with some officers, to receive me. The men presented arms, and some of the officers shook hands with me. I made my best bow, and that, I fear, a bad one, for I felt in a very strange and uncomfortable situation. There were, of course, many spectators. I just thanked them for their kind and dutiful attention, and walking to the head of the wharf found Lady Harvey's carriage waiting to convey me to Government House. Into this I entered with the two clergymen and in about 7 or 8 minutes had passed through the town and was landed at Government House. At the door, Sir John Harvey, the Governor, received me and introduced me to Lady Harvey. The family, I found, consisted at this time of Sir John and Lady Harvey, Mr. Harvey, the Governor's eldest son and secretary, and his wife, the daughter (Ella) of my predecessor [Bishop Spencer][3] with their baby, a year old. Lieut Harvey, the Governor's youngest son, and Capt. Elliot of HMS *Euridice*. Dr. Henry, who had accompanied us from Halifax, was also received into the house. Mr. Bridge, Mr. Blackman and Palairet dined with the Governor at 7 o'clock, and we retired to rest at 10 o'clock,

[1]Construction of the Roman Catholic cathedral was begun with the excavation of the ground in 1839. The cornerstone was laid in 1841, but it was not completed and consecrated until 1855.

[2]The Royal Newfoundland Companies formed the imperial garrison in St. John' s from 1824 to1862.

[3]Aubrey George Spencer (1795-1872), a great-great-grandson of John Churchill, 1st Duke of Marlborough. Spencer had married Eliza Musson, daughter of a wealthy Bermuda merchant, by whom he had one son and three daughters.

Palairet being entertained at the Bridges, I remaining at the Governor's very kindly cared for and comfortably lodged.

Such was my introduction to my new diocese: not, it is too manifest, in very primitive or apostolic style, yet so I should hope as not to give offence to any high-minded Christians. The respect and ceremony were shown to me and accepted by me as a bishop of the Church, and though I would have preferred a procession with litanies and holy services and priests and choristers, yet where none could be found to make or understand them, the mixture of ecclesiastical with secular ceremony was not contemptuously to be rejected. To me individually, it was very distasteful, but that helped to reconcile me to it and made me hope it might be of use to others, if God please. May He pardon my weakness and ignorance, and if He sees that such respects are not sought or desired by me, as I trust is the case, may He graciously prevent injury from them to me or the cause which I am sent to serve. Amen.

Friday, July 5

Was waited on after breakfast (which is at 10 o'clock) by Mr. Bridge and Blackman and a few other inhabitants and officers.

Was glad to find that there is a service at the parish church at 7 o'clock every Friday. Of course, determined to go. Palairet came to luncheon at 2 o'clock. Went to the house of the ex-Chief Justice [Hon. J.G.H. Bourne], who has just been dismissed, and directed the auctioneer to purchase some of his goods at the sale. Examined the house occupied by the late Bishop, which is to be my residence at least for a time. Dark and dismal, without any garden and very ill-provided with servants' apartments &c. In the evening, went to Mr. Bridge's house and drank tea with him before the service at 7 o'clock. Palairet said the service. Mr. Blackman preached. An amazing disunity, full of flowers of rhetoric and delivered in a bombastic style — quite new to me. The matter and manner were so strange as to seem almost ludicrous. The clerk's voice and manner were equally new and strange, and the smell of fish in the church was strong and by no means agreeable. The church itself is old, ugly, dusty, dirty and dismal.

Saturday, July 6

Occupied this morning in writing a sermon. At twelve o'clock waited upon by the officers of the Royal Newfoundland Companies, to whom I made my acknowledgements for their attendance and attention on my landing. Visited also by Major Robe, Mr. B. Robinson and others.

Dined at 7 o'clock and met several officers and members of the Council. Ladies in the evening who sang and played — among others a Miss Law sang nicely — *indoctum sed dulce*.[4] Finished my sermon after 10 o'clock.

[4]Horace, *Epistles*, 2: 2: *Indoctum sed dulce* — unpolished but pleasant.

Sunday, July 7

Directly after breakfast, went in Lady Harvey's carriage to St. John's Church, where I preached and, assisted by Mr. Bridge, administered the Holy Sacrament to nearly 150 communicants. Church pretty well attended but not full. Alms collected in shabby wooden and copper boxes at the end of sticks, and these one after the other presented by myself on the Holy Table. It was next to impossible to bring them reverently or present them humbly. I preached from the gospel of the day, St. Luke 5: 4-5.[5] The wine was under the table in a black bottle, no flagon. Service was concluded about half past or 20 minutes past two o'clock.

At three o'clock, went to St. Thomas's Church, where I preached from . . . . Mr. Blackman said the prayers. Church not full. Sir John Harvey and Capt. Elliot only from Government House. Dined at Government House at 7 o'clock. The family party only. Received a note after I had retired from Sir J. Harvey, regretting he had not asked for prayers and requesting some might be read every morning.

Monday, July 8

At 10 o'clock said some of the Prayers of the Church. Present Sir John and Lady Harvey, Mr. and Mrs. Harvey, and Dr. Henry — none of the servants.

Employed after breakfast in writing letters for England till one o'clock. At one o'clock received an address from the Rector, churchwardens and vestry of St. John's Church. About 30 gentlemen attended. Mr. Bridge read the address, which I acknowledged and replied to as well as I could and, as it was without any preparation, badly enough. At ¼ past one came Mr. Blackman in his clerical costume with about 6 of his vestry on a similar errand. To these I made a suitable reply. Called on Mrs. Carrington, the widow of the penultimate Rector [Rev. Frederick Carrington], who has a large family which she finds some difficulty in providing for and maintaining. One son, her eldest, is at the college at Windsor, 19 years of age, a scapegrace. The second is at Clergy Orphan School, St. John's Road, London — a promising lad.

At four o'clock, Sir John Harvey took me in his carriage through the town along a newly formed road to a place called Waterford Bridge, about 4 miles from the town. The road lies at the bottom of a ravine or valley, along which runs the little river or brook which falls into the harbour. On the north side, the lands are well cultivated and on either and both sides pretty in position and shape, but sadly in need of wood. Nothing but the most stunted, miserable fir trees and but few even of these. The sides of the valley not unlike the banks of the Wye opposite near Weir, if you could but clothe them with gardens and wood. I saw large herds of goats browsing

[5]Luke 5: 4-5: Now when he had left speaking, he said unto Simon, Launch out into the deep, and let down your nets for a draught. And Simon answering said until him, Master, we have toiled all the night, and have taken nothing: nevertheless at thy word I will let down the net.

on the South Side, probably 150 in number together. The road very good as far as we went.

On our return, Sir John kindly proposed a walk, and we went accordingly round Quidi Vidi Lake, about 3 miles, round which a carriage road is in course of formation, promising hereafter to be a fashionable drive, and when the sides of the lake are planted, pretty. The Hyde Park of St. John's. Went through a part of Quidi Vidi Station, which is a mere fishing station with a little church. Saw a cartload of capelin which were going to be used as manure. In several places, the country smelt very strongly of the fish manure, which consists chiefly of the heads of the codfish mixed with bog-earth. Some nice farms on either side of the Quidi Vidi Lake.

A large dinner and evening party — Capitaine Fabvre[6] of a French corvette [*la Fortune*] and many gentlemen of St. John's at dinner. The other officers of the French ship and those of the *Eurydice* came in the evening with many ladies — music and dancing. I retired at 11 o'clock, and the party separated soon after 12 o'clock. Mr. Bridge dined.

Tuesday, July 9

Only Sir John and Lady Harvey at prayers at 10 o'clock. A small muster indeed! At eleven walked with Palairet to Signal Hill and had much talk with him — found him independent and contrary. Visited a school at the Barracks on the hill, the master of which is a sergeant — nearly 90 children on the books. The school was dispersed as the master was on the parade. Returned to lunch at 2½ o'clock. On my way from Signal Hill called on Mr. Dunscombe, the father of Mrs. Bridge. Called on Mr. Bridge at 5½ o'clock.

At 7 o'clock accompanied the Governor to dinner at Fort Townshend by invitation from the officers of the R. Newfoundland Companies. The dinner in their mess room at the Barracks — 34 present, and of these about 24 wore epaulettes, being either military or naval officers. Capt. Elliot with the officers of HMS *Eurydice* and Capitaine Fabvre with some of his officers were among the number, the others military. Mr. Blackman and I the only clergy.

Wednesday, July 10

Only Sir John and Lady Harvey at prayers. At 11 o'clock went with Mr. and Mrs. Bridge and Palairet in Mr. Bridge's carriage to Portugal Cove, one of the out-harbours of St. John's, 9½ miles from the Capital. The road is nearly new and for the most part very good, none very bad — none such as presented any difficulty to a double-bodied phaeton drawn by one horse and containing four persons. Some of the hills are steep, and on this account we walked up them, but not because the

[6]Jean-Jacques-Louis Fabvre (1800-1864).

roads were deep or ill-made. For the two first miles from St. John's the land on either side of the road is enclosed and cultivated, chiefly as pasture, and many decent, comfortable houses and cottages are seen. We then came into the low forests of fir or of pine, not generally exceeding 7 or 8 feet in height and proportionally small. These are probably a second growth, former forests having been cut down or destroyed by fire, but they have been many years reaching their present diminutive size. In these forests, and especially near the sides of the road, are many solitary houses, all, it is believed, with one exception, occupied by Roman Catholics. These, from within 4 or 5 miles of St. John's, attend the service at their chapel in the Capital with exemplary regularity. We passed between two lakes or ponds about 3 or 4 miles from St. John's and a little further skirted a larger one called 20-Mile Pond, being, it is supposed, 20 miles in circumference. The extremity of this farthest from St. John's is very pretty and picturesque, dotted with little islands which are covered with the short fir trees in elegant groups.

The approach to Portugal Cove is by a steep descent through broken rocks and rockeries of the most picturesque appearance, having fir trees and other shrubs growing out of the clefts and on their sides and summits. Immense boulders lie on the sides of the hills and in the ravines and are sometimes gathered into fields together in masses which on a large scale represent the most perfect specimens of rockeries such as are attempted in gardens and parks.

In descending towards the village, the little wooden church is a conspicuous and interesting object. It is built on a rocky ledge of a very steep and lofty hill, of course near the base, and the churchyard is very much broken and diversified. The chief and great objection to the locality is that being a mere rock it is very difficult and almost impossible to dig graves. The dead bodies, in fact, are not laid more than one foot under the surface, and a very distressing consequence has lately been that dogs scratched up and partly ate the corpse of a young man buried there. The church was built through the exertions of Archdeacon Wix and is very sufficiently provided with furniture of all kinds, except of course Communion plate.

Near to the church is a school supported by the Newfoundland School Society,[7] which we entered and found upwards of 40 children of both sexes assembled under the management of a respectable young man and woman who have lived many years, nearly their whole lives, in Newfoundland. The woman indeed is a native. They receive between £50 a year currency, with a dwelling house. Both the church and school are requiring repairs. The latter is represented as very cold in winter, for want of what is called cieling [*sic*] — that is, inside boarding not on the roof only but the walls. Both church and school are supported by posts, which soon decay. A conspicuous object from the school and church is the Methodist meeting house,

[7]The Newfoundland School Society was established in 1823 by the merchant Samuel Codner (1776-1858). The first NSS school appeared in St. John's in 1823, and the demand spread rapidly to rural Newfoundland, where petitions and applications for schools were made. Within ten years, 43 schools had been established.

larger, apparently, than the church, and at a little distance is the Roman Catholic chapel, well placed, well built and in good repair.

There is no resident clergyman of any persuasion or denomination, and the prayers of the Church, and afterwards a sermon, are read by the schoolmaster. There are said to be between 300 and 400 Protestants in the cove, all fishermen, all poor. Roads are in course of construction and improvement, and packets sail every day to Carbonear or Harbour Grace. The whole cove is set round with fish flakes — and of course, at this season, redolent of fish. At a little distance is Belle Isle [Bell Island], where is also a church but no clergyman. There are two chief settlements on this island, one entirely of Romanists, the other chiefly of Protestants. The island itself is represented as fertile.

We had a very good dinner of salmon and ham at the little inn and returned by the way we came to attend a meeting of the Church Society in St. John's. It was held at the upper room of the Newfoundland Schools. Several persons attended, male and female. Mr. Bridge read some of the Prayers of the Church and addressed the people. I also spoke a few words, and then Mr. Bridge read some extracts from quarterly papers of the S.P.G., and I dismissed them with the Blessing. Subscriptions in arrears were paid up and a collection made.

Thursday, July 11

At one o'clock this morning [*sic*] went on board the French ship (la *Fortune*) to acknowledge a call from the Captain — Fabvre. This ship is sent out by the French government to protect their fisheries on the coast of Newfoundland, and the Captain has this year a commission to negotiate some alterations in the treaties between England and France relating to this subject. He is an open, plain, intelligent person, very much like an old English naval officer. His ship is in beautiful order — and great attention seems to be paid to the sick. No chaplain on board and no religious service.

After visiting this ship, I went on board the *Eurydice* (Capt. Elliot), a much more elegant ship and better sailor.[8] The captain's cabin is very nicely arranged and fitted up, but I missed the hospital for the sick. There are 240 men on board this ship, and she is considered a very beautiful vessel. No chaplain. Dined at Government House.

[8]HMS *Eurydice*, launched in 1843, was a 921-ton, 26-gun frigate with a sleek wooden hull and a broad expanse of sail. She was considered to be one of the finest vessels in the Royal Navy. In 1876, she underwent a routine refit at Cowes. Since ironclads such as HMS *Warrior* had made wooden warships obsolete, she was then converted into a training vessel but was lost at sea in 1878.

Friday, July 12

At 11½ o'clock, I married in St. Thomas's Church Lieut. Heathcote, RN, of the *Eurydice* to Miss Law, eldest daughter of Col. Law, who is the Commanding Officer of the Royal Newfoundland Companies. Sir John and Lady Harvey attended and a great number of friends and spectators. At 1½ o'clock, I went with Sir John and Lady Harvey to a *déjeuner* [lunch] at Col. Law's house in barracks at Fort Townshend. Remained about half an hour. Went in the evening to St. John's Church. Palairet read prayers and Mr. Bridge preached a long sermon from a long text. Very wet day.

Saturday, July 13

Got the furniture purchased at the Chief Justice's sale into the house I have taken for a year. Met Palairet there and persuaded him to make some arrangements for my housekeeping. Wrote a sermon and dined with Sir John and Lady and Mr. Harvey. Mrs. Harvey ill from the effects of yesterday's amusements.

Sunday, July 14

At 11 o'clock went to St. Thomas's Church, where I preached. Sir John and Lady Harvey attended. In the afternoon, I preached at St. John's. The Governor and Capt. Elliot walked down with me to the church. After the service, I took a walk with Palairet at the back of the Roman Catholic Cathedral and then to his lodgings.

Dined at Government House. Capt. Elliot and a Capt. Bailey of RNC dined. Read one of Bishop Blomfield's prayers[9] at 9 o'clock. Had notice given of daily prayers at St. Thomas's at 9½ o'clock. At St. Thomas's Church a noisy clerk and dumb congregation and nearly the same at St. John's.

Monday, July 15

Commenced Morning Prayers in St. Thomas's Church at 9½ o'clock. Sir John Harvey accompanied me, and I sat in his pew. More than 20 in attendance besides the students and clergy.

At 12 o'clock attended a meeting of the building committee of the projected cathedral. Found them and their affairs in great confusion. Plans wretched, money

[9]Charles James Blomfield (1786-1857), Bishop of Chester and subsequently Bishop of London, took a leading position in the action for church reform which culminated in the Ecclesiastical Commission and did much for the extension of the colonial episcopate. He was an invaluable mediator in the controversies arising out of the Tractarian Movement. His published works consist of charges, sermons, lectures and pamphlets and a manual of private and family prayers. See G. E. Biber, *Bishop Blomfield and his Times* (1857).

exhausted and debts already incurred. I persuaded the committee to let me send the drawings &c to England to obtain opinions and instructions. After the meeting went over the old church with Mr. Bridge and Palairet and suggested several alterations, among others to move the pulpit from the centre of the church against the gallery, the erection of a bishop's seat, a font, &c.

At 5 o'clock, walked out with Bridge and Palairet and dined at the Governor's at 7 o'clock with the same.

Tuesday, July 16

Prayers in church at 9 o'clock. Mr. Blackman officiated. Wrote and wasted my time after breakfast till 2 o'clock. At 3 o'clock went to my new house and determined on some alterations and additions. Made some calls and walked with Palairet to Quidi Vidi. Beautiful day and the scenery about Quidi Vidi and the lake quite lovely. The mouth of Quidi Vidi harbour so narrow as to admit only boats. The flakes covered with fish. Examined the church, which is simple but sufficient, if there were any ventilation. The surplices thrown about in a very careless manner. One was wrapped round the Bible and prayer books, and so thrown on the altar. Wet comes in at one corner.

Dined at Government House, met the Greens and French officers. Lilacs and laburnums in first blossom. Peas in blossom, no young potatoes, a few strawberries just coming on, no gooseberries or currants ripe. Grass not ready to cut.

Wednesday, July 17

Palairet said the prayers at St. Thomas's Church, a good deal too slow, and the lessons with too much effect as though he were acting the part of the speakers. Had a long visit from the Rev. Mr. [William] Hoyles, the missionary at Ferryland, who is anxious to be ordained priest. After much consultation and consideration, thought it best to defer the ordination till the canonical time in the month of September. Much pleased with his earnest manner and the [acumen] of his simple mode of life.

Received visits from a Mr. Wilson, Mr. Rendell, Mr. Prowse.

Went with Mr. Bridge and Palairet to make some calls and afterwards took a walk and examined the Roman Catholic Cathedral, an immense pile of building but without any pretensions to ecclesiastical propriety. There is an ambulatory all about the building, partly, I suppose, for processions and partly to protect the interior structure and its inmates from the weather. The thickness of the interior walls which support the roof is 4 feet and of the walls of the ambulatory 3. The ambulatory has a lean-to covering. Dined at Government House and met Mr. Blackman and his son-in-law, Lieut. Talbot.

Thursday, July 18

In the morning made calls with Mr. Bridge and Palairet. Dined at the house of Mr. William Thomas, the churchwarden of St. John's Church. At 7 o'clock the *North America* steamer from Halifax arrived, bringing the mail from England, an event of universal interest to the inhabitants of St. John's and not least to myself. The mail arrived in 14 days from England, having left Liverpool on the 4th of July, the day of my arrival at St. John's, Nfld.

Friday, July 19

Said the prayers myself at St. Thomas's Church, a great delight which I have long missed. Wrote letters all the morning. Went to the evening service at St. John's Church. Mr. Hoyles preached, plain and colloquial and too much in the old presumptuous way of justification.[10]

Saturday, July 20

Wrote letters nearly all day for the packet tomorrow. Had a letter and visit from the Rev. Mr. [H.J.] Fitzgerald, Rural Dean of Trinity, with many appeals for assistance in building churches in his district.

Sunday, July 21

Started at 8½ o'clock with Mr. Bridge for Torbay. My robes were put in a tin box, which was put in a small Nova Scotia waggon on 2 wheels with a seat for two persons, drawn by one horse, value of the same about £7. My servant, Mr. Bridge's man, mounted the same and rode all the way to Torbay. Mr. Bridge and I walked the whole way, 7½ miles. The road is in course of formation, sufficient made for horses and for pedestrians in dry weather, very rough in places for a carriage, but our waggon got along without much difficulty. The road runs a considerable way nearly parallel to and not far distant from the road to Portugal Cove. It is taken through the thick woods of small and stunted fir which are found all over this part of the island. The roads are easily made, as the materials are abundant; the substratum is generally dry and admits of draining.

[10]In Christian theology, justification is regarded as God's act making a sinner righteous. However, the means and scope of justification are areas of significant debate. Catholics and Orthodox Christians distinguish between initial justification, which occurs at baptism, and final justification, which is accomplished after a lifetime of striving to do God's will. Protestants believe that justification is a singular act in which God declares an unrighteous individual to be righteous because of the work of Jesus.

There are no lofty hills to be lowered or valleys to be filled up and no large trees to be rooted up. The chief difficulty and expense seem to be in filling up occasional morasses or marshy places, which is done by throwing trees in them and covering these first with boughs and then with the stone and gravel. We passed near Virginia Water on the right hand side going down, and on our left hand and nearly opposite was some of the Church land. On our way, we were overtaken by one of the Romish priests on a nice grey pony going from St. John's to Torbay to attend the chapel there. His name was Forristall,[11] and he begged to be introduced to me, and descending from his pony he took off his hat, held out his hand and said, "Welcome, my Lord, to Newfoundland."

The settlement of Torbay is populous, upwards of 800 souls, of whom 200 only are members of our church, the rest all Romanists. The cottages of the settlers are situated on the sides of two gentle but widely extended declivities bare of wood and without any large rocks but with a broken and undulating surface. Small enclosures fenced by low stone walls are very numerous and give an impression favourable of the habits of the people, of their industry and prospects. The bay was filled with small fishing boats, and there is a small beach of pebbles very much like that of Babbicombe [Bay]. The hills on either side of the bay also reminded me of Babbicombe, being of nearly the same size and colour and very green on the summit. This is the first beach I have seen since I left England and the first place where I could conveniently approach the sea to dip my fingers into its waters.

The Roman Catholic chapel is on the hill as you approach Torbay from St. John's, very nicely situated among some trees, well built and maintained. The bell is on a pole in front of the building but separate from it and covered with a canopy — at the other end and against the building is a small apartment for the priest where he breakfasts after the service. We saw a large number of exceedingly well dressed men and women (the men chiefly in sailors' costume) assembled near the chapel or mounting the sides of the hill towards it. Some of them bowed and saluted us, but more looked scorn and defiance. As we wound down the hill by a narrow footpath where our cart could not follow us, my robe box was taken from the cart by my servant and carried after us. Mr. Bridge's servant took care of the horse and carriage and was directed to go to the Roman Catholic chapel, he being of that communion.

Our church is at the bottom of the hill very near the beach and is a simple, neat wooden structure erected chiefly through the exertions of Mr. Bridge. I found a very decent congregation assembled, and having first visited the school (which belongs to the Newfoundland School Society and is maintained at their expense during the week, where we found 17 scholars, boys and girls, and two of the theological students assisting), we proceeded to the service.

[11]Rev. John Forristall was the administrator of the Roman Catholic parish in St. John's, 1838-1850. At this time, the parish church was located on Henry Street. His major occupation was overseeing the construction of the Cathedral.

The church is fitted up with open benches only, with 2 pulpits, one for praying and the other for preaching, a small, decent altar with very little space enclosed by rails. A chancel is in course of erection through the liberality of Mr. Thomas, who gave £15 for that purpose. Mr. Bridge said the prayers and baptized a child and churched the mother[12] after the 2nd lesson. The woman, I afterwards found, was a Roman Catholic. I was much pleased with the little congregation about 100 in number and regretted I was not provided with a discourse more suited to their condition and capacity. Notice was given that whenever I should again attend, the Holy Communion would be administered.

We left about one o'clock and took our way back again. Mr. Bridge provided me with a biscuit, and we called at the cottage of a member of our church and congregation who lived about 3 miles from Torbay to ask for a glass of water. They produced a nice jug of milk and two glass tumblers. The family consisted of a man and daughter who had accompanied us to and from the church, the man's wife and daughter-in-law and son and 2 grandchildren. The house was surrounded by wood, or nearly so, but not far from the road, like one of the cottages in the Forest of Dean, with a clearing round it, very rudely built and ill-protected against the cold, the walls not being cieled. There was, however, an ample fireplace with a chimney corner like those of the cottages and farmhouses in Oxfordshire, where the family could creep for shelter and warmth. On either side of this were the mistress and his daughter-in-law.

When we arrived within 2 miles or 2½ miles of St. John's, we got into the little cart and drove on, leaving our servants, in order to reach Quidi Vidi by 3 o'clock for the afternoon service. Here I put on my robes in a fisherman's cottage near the church and walked thence to the church. Mr. Bridge said the prayers, and I preached. This church [is] also due to Mr. Bridge's exertions, neat and simple, only provided with forms [benches] at present, a pulpit, reading seat and altar, without rails. About 75 persons present. We returned to St. John's in our little waggon by 5 o'clock. Dined at Government House: new potatoes and strawberries today for the first time and considered early. No raspberries, currants or gooseberries yet up — no peas or French beans. Lilacs and laburnums still in bloom.

The mail left at 7 o'clock for Halifax, to proceed to England on the 3rd of next month.

Monday, July 22

A very wet day and took advantage of it to write out a draft of a report for the church building committee of the progress and prospects of the cathedral. Had a visit from Mr. Bridge and a long conference with the Rev. H.J. Fitzgerald, whom I endeavoured to dispose to better views of church matters, material and moral.

[12]The Churching of Women: a ceremony wherein a blessing is given to a mother after childbirth.

Wrote a long letter to him relating to his applications for assistance in building new churches &c and gave him notice of my intention to hold a visitation on the 21st of September and an ordination on the following Sunday, requesting him to notify the same to the clergy of his deanery.

Tuesday, July 23

Prayers at 9½ o'clock. Walked with Mr. Blackman and Palairet to make calls. Heard of the arrival of the *Mary and Anne* with my Bicknor goods. Dined at Government House. Received a complaint against the Rev. Mr. [J.M.] Martine [Rector of Brigus].

Wednesday, July 24

Sent letters by the *Swallow* to Rev. E. Hawkins and Revd. R. Davies. Rode with Mr. Bridge to Petty Harbour, about 10 miles distant from St. John's. The road lies through the town, then along the western bank of the river through a very pleasing, pretty country leading to an extensive valley which appears fertile and productive or likely to become so. Through this valley lies the new road to the Bay of Bulls. The road to Petty Harbour turns to the left and lies through the most rugged, rocky country that can be conceived. The hills on either side of the road are covered with immense boulders, lying in ruin and confusion — confusion worse confounded.[13] These are generally split, probably by the action of the frost. The hills in this neighbourhood are generally bare and having only these rude, impracticable masses, split and tossed about in wild array or else in and among these boulders stumps of small trees which have been destroyed by fires. Where the trees grow and remain, the hills and ravines are pretty and picturesque and are much set off by the numerous lakes and ponds, of which there are 8 or 10 on different sides of the road.

The road is only now in course of formation, and we were obliged to leave our horses or at least dismount them about 2 miles from Petty Harbour, just as we came in sight of the sea, and make our way as we could through and over the bogs and boulders and descend some very steep, stony hills to the little settlement. It is a complete fishing settlement, the hills on either side being so rocky as not to admit of gardens, as there are at Torbay. The flakes are very extensive, running up a valley down which descends a shallow broad stream. This stream or river divides the settlement, and on one side are exclusively Romanists, probably 700 or more, and on the other side almost exclusively members of our Church, between 300 and 400 in number. No Dissenters.

The Roman Catholic chapel is substantial and in good repair but is surpassed by the Church, which is just new (replacing an old one) and only just finished exter-

[13]John Milton, *Paradise Lost* (1667), 2: 995-96: With ruin upon ruin, rout on rout,/Confusion worse confounded.

nally. The interior arrangements not commenced. It is very roomy and convenient and might be fitted up to look very nicely if one had money and taste. It is built on land belonging to the Newfoundland School Society, not yet conveyed to the Church. The school is close by and appears to be well managed by a young man names Earles (son of the clerk of St. John's Church). There were 60 blooming, beautiful children in attendance — the girls rather too smart — with plaited hair and ornamented bonnets and many of the boys without shoes, but on the whole well and properly dressed.

The evening was lovely, and we did not leave till 4½ o'clock — got to St. John's by six o'clock, drank tea at Mr. Bridge's, where I met Mrs. Bennett and her sister and went to prayers at the church at 7 o'clock, being the eve or vigil of St. James. It is remarkable that wherever the firs are destroyed by fire in the woods, raspberry bushes immediately grow up and cover the ground. Where the fires have not been, as in the boggy and marshy ground, are groves of hurtleberries [blueberries] and the Indian tea, interspersed with calmias and other low shrubs.

Thursday, July 25, St. James's Day

Went to St. John's Church at 11 o'clock and read the Communion Service and prayer for the Church Militant.[14] Mr. Bridge preached. After the service examined the church with a view to the projected alterations and improvements with a Mr. Purcell,[15] a supposed builder, an unimaginative Irishman — after made calls on several persons. A large party at Government House at dinner, among others a Mr. [Thomas] Ridley, the chief merchant of Harbour Grace and a member of the [Executive] Council,[16] Col. Law, Lieut. and Mrs. Heathcote &c — returned at 10 o'clock.

Friday, July 26

Said the prayers at St. Thomas's Church. Had a visit from Mr. Blackman about seats in St. Thomas's Church for the accommodation of the military — could not come to any conclusion. Made calls with Mr. Bridge. Received an invitation to dinner for

[14]The Church Militant: Christians who are living, as opposed to the Church Triumphant, comprising those who are in Heaven.

[15]James Purcell, an Irish stonecutter and masonry contractor, had been engaged by the Roman Catholic bishop to superintend construction of his cathedral. During the 1840s, Purcell was also involved in the construction of public buildings, including the Colonial Building. But having purchased a number of properties on speculation, he became insolvent and left Newfoundland in 1858.

[16]From 1820 to 1870, Thomas Ridley was one of the most important merchants in Newfoundland. During an attempt to become elected to the House of Assembly in 1836, he was forced to withdraw because of violence and intimidation. In 1840 he was nearly killed during his second attempt to obtain a seat. Eventually, he managed to get elected, and he served on the Executive Council from 1843 until 1848.

Friday next at Mr. H. Thomas. Refused because Fridays are to be observed as fasts. Went to St. John's Church in the evening. Mr. Bridge preached. Luggage all landed at my house.

Saturday, July 27

Wrote to Miss Davies before breakfast to announce the arrival of my packages. Started at 8½ o'clock with Mr. Bridge for Harbour Grace. Mr. Bridge drove me in his carriage to Portugal Cove, where we were joined by Mr. Ridley, the merchant of Harbour Grace. We reached Portugal Cove by 10¼ o'clock — waiting there for a packet to convey us to Harbour Grace, we encountered a Mr. Pitts, a planter of Belle Isle [Bell Island], who offered to present the members of our church at Portugal Cove with a small piece of land for a cemetery, having witnessed with pain a funeral a few days before in the present churchyard, where it is nearly impossible to cover a coffin on account of the rocky nature of the ground. I accepted the gift for the Church and made my acknowledgements. The old gentleman informed us that he keeps in his possession a piece of cedar wood from Mount Lebanon, wishing and intending to make from it a pulpit for the little church at Belle Isle, which alas! never sees a clergyman.

We left Portugal Cove at quarter past eleven and had what is called a "fine time" passing over the bay to Harbour Grace in less than four hours, the winds light and a calm sea. The day was very fine, and the various bays, islands and coasts were shining brightly. Approaching Harbour Grace, we see the scattered houses of the town of Carbonear lying upon the side of a bleak, desolate hill: the whole coast presents the like appearance, bleak and barren beyond all my powers of description. The entrance to Harbour Grace is hidden for a time by Harbour Grace Island, a large rock on which is a wooden lighthouse. Passing this island, we saw the harbour and town before us. The harbour is a long, commodious bay, having a somewhat dangerous shoal at the entrance, but after that is passed deep and safe.

We landed at Mr. Ridley's wharf, where several of the principal inhabitants (somewhat rusty and colonial but respectable and well informed) had come to meet and greet me. We arrived at Mr. Ridley's house, which is a neat stone building, the only dwelling of stone, I believe, in Harbour Grace,[17] by 3 o'clock. I was introduced there to Mrs. Ridley. They have 4 sons at school in Liverpool.

We visited the church, which is the only stone one on the island and certainly makes me fear that stone churches are not likely to succeed for some generations to come. It was built during the residence of the Rev. Mr. [John] Burt[18] and after the great fire which destroyed the former church and almost the whole town in 1832. It is already much out of repair, and the stones of the arches of the windows in the tower are quite shattered by the frost. A vestry has been added to the building at the

[17]Built in 1834, Ridley Hall is made of local stone and brick with a slate roof.
[18]Rev. John Burt was the missionary at Harbour Grace, 1821-40.

east end, to which a door of communication has been made through the wall; another has caused a rent and fissure. The tower, which appears to have been built after and added to the nave of the church, has considerably separated from it, and altogether the state of repair externally is bad. The cracks at the east end are visible inside, and otherwise the interior appearance, both of the walls and seats, is unsatisfactory.

The arrangement of the seats is nearly the same as in St. Thomas's Church in the Capital — a block of long pews in the middle with a passage on either side and between these passages and the walls and under the galleries two blocks of shorter pews. The galleries occupy 3 sides of the church as in St. John's: but the arrangement of pulpit, reading pew and Communion table is novel and extraordinary indeed. At the east end of the church are two single light windows at equal distances from the north and south walls respectively, leaving a blank space in the centre of the east wall, where the east window is usually found. Immediately against this space and in the centre of it towers the pulpit — in front of this, conveniently depressed, the reading desk, and again in front of the reading desk the Communion table, over which hangs and projects the desk of the reading pew. The whole is surrounded by a circular rail at which the communicants kneel, so that (in the language of the country) you go through the Communion table, or a Communion, to go to the reading pew and pulpit. This arrangement was introduced by the Revd. Mr. Burt, missionary at Harbour Grace when this church was built, and was carried to all the neighbouring churches subsequently erected. It is common, I had heard, in Ireland.

This church is vested by deed in 9 trustees who are empowered to let out the seats by annual rents, but by the deed 50 seats are to be reserved and kept for the poor. These, however, have been taken and let out as pews, and to increase the number of sittings 4 rows of benches have been put in the gallery, where originally were built but three, and they confined enough.

I preached and administered the Sacrament in this church in the morning (62 communicants). It was but too evident (unless I was much mistaken) that the congregation and people are in a very unsatisfactory state. Their last missionary, the Revd. Mr. [George B.] Cowan, died a short time only before my arrival. He appears to have been an amiable man but not at all calculated to minister among a worldly and ill-instructed and encroaching people. The parsonage house is in a state of ruin and utterly unfit for the residence of a clergyman, or indeed of any person.

There is a large Roman Catholic chapel and also a Wesleyan meeting house in the town. There was a great fire in the town just before my arrival at St. John's, 24 dwellings and stores quite destroyed. A few years ago (in 1832) almost the whole town was burnt, and it is remarkable that the fire this time commenced where the former had ceased, so that the entire street has been cleared. An excellent street 50 ft. wide is now laid out, and the airy and spacious appearance of the town, in consequence, is very pleasing. There is a long, wide promenade or street with houses on the north side only, extending along the bay into the country to the east, which reminded me very much of Budleigh Salterton [Devon].

After the morning service, Mr. Ridley drove myself and Mr. Bridge in his carriage to Carbonear, a town populous and once flourishing, about 3 miles from Harbour Grace. The road lies over bleak hills, either entirely bare or clothed in parts with the low, stunted fir. After ascending a very steep, stony ridge from Hr. Grace, you descend towards Carbonear and see the harbour lying before you, running like that of Hr. Grace into the interior, though not so high up. The town or settlement lies widely scattered on the north side of the harbour on a bleak, barren slope. I remembered the letter of "Senex", who told me that if ever I reached a place called Carbonear I should wish myself back in England. I certainly felt very sad, as I did for some unknown reason, the whole day, but not from any dread or dislike of the country.

The day was bright and beautiful and though nothing can be more barren and desolate than the country, yet the houses are comfortable, the roads decent and the inhabitants well dressed. If I had been an unconcerned or common spectator, I might have been even pleased by the outward appearance of the town, but I beheld and lo! a large Roman Catholic chapel in the valley and half way up the hill a still larger Methodist meeting house. Here are the headquarters of the Wesleyans and their loftiest, largest meeting house. The church of wood is on the hill, nearer the top and the smallest of the three "ecclesiastical" buildings. It is, however, nicely situated, and the churchyard is well fenced. The arrangements of the interior are similar to those of Harbour Grace, except that there are no side galleries, and the vestry is in the tower on a level with the gallery and approached by the same staircase, which is exceedingly disagreeable.

I preached to a pretty full congregation, one third of whom, however, I was told, were Wesleyans. The Rev. Mr. [James] Harvey is the clergyman, appointed by Bishop Spencer. He is married for the 2nd time to a Miss Pack, the daughter of a principal merchant at Carbonear. He seems a well-meaning young man but not endowed with great powers either bodily or mental. He swells out his reading in the colonial style, which seems particularly absurd coming from so diminutive a subject. Would he were fatter! After the service, I went to the parsonage, a house bought for the clergyman a short time ago, considerably too far from the church but otherwise sufficient and suitable. There I was introduced to Mrs. Harvey and Mrs. Lind, the wife of a missionary at Heart's Content [Rev. Henry Lind], and to a leg of mutton. All and each of which were pleasing in their way.

Mr. Ridley drove us back to Hr. Grace in time for the evening service, where Mr. [John] Kingwell, the deacon and schoolmaster, said the prayers and Mr. Bridge preached. Mr. Kingwell is the master of the Newfoundland School at Hr. Grace and was ordained deacon by Bishop Spencer. He continues to act as schoolmaster at Hr. Grace and has the charge of 2 churches, at Island Cove and Bishop's Cove, and since Mr. Cowan's death officiates also at Hr. Grace — and has only one leg! I went into the Sunday School at Hr. Grace and was very unfavourably impressed both with the matter and manners of the teaching there. Mrs. Kingwell, the wife of the schoolmaster and herself the schoolmistress, died a short time since, and Miss Kingwell, the daughter, occupies her post, and I was not pleased with this young lady. She behaved lightly at the Sacrament.

Monday, July 29

After breakfast, I was waited on by a deputation from the Church inhabitants of Hr. Grace who read and presented an address congratulating me on my arrival among them, representing the destitute state of their church and town and begging me to provide a clergyman, suggesting that the Revd. Mr. [H.J.] Fitzgerald of Trinity would be acceptable. I replied at some length, calling their attention to the state of the church and churchyard fence, the malapropriation [*sic*] of the 50 reserved seats for the poor, which I desired might be restored to their proper use, and the ruinous state of the parsonage, promising towards a new one £75, viz. £25 at the commencement, £50 when finished, and with respect to Mr. Fitzgerald saying that as he was both usefully and comfortably placed I did not think I ought to remove him for the benefit of Hr. Grace but that it was as much my desire as my duty to provide a clergyman for the station as soon as possible.

At 10 o'clock I started with Mr. Bridge and Mr. Kingwell on horseback for Island Cove and Bishop's Cove, two settlements with churches about 8 miles from Harbour Grace. The road is in course of formation through the usual fir forests in which are several bogs which a few years ago would have let in a horse up to his belly or higher; they are now partly covered with the felled trunks of the trees on the line of road, but we were obliged to go over them with caution. On nearing the settlement of Island Cove, we descended, as usual, towards the sea, between and round some highly picturesque rocks. The settlement is a large one, entirely devoted to fishing pursuits, with a few gardens in the immediate vicinity. The people are chiefly members of our church, and a more interesting race in appearance and behaviour could rarely, I think, be found. Though the fishing was at its height and a very promising season had commenced after long waiting and disappointment, there was a large attendance both of men and women at the church. I have not seen a more interesting or apparently interested congregation.

I addressed them without notes on the text "By their fruits ye shall know them"[19] and endeavoured to shew what are fruits necessary or expected in a Christian that he may be known as such, the sad consequences of not bringing forth good fruit and the means or ways by which Christians are made and continued fruitful, viz. by the word of God and the sacraments. I explained also the object and purpose of my being sent and coming among them, viz. to provide and take care that the

[19]Matthew 7: 19-20: Every tree that bringeth not forth good fruit is hewn down, and cast into the fire. Wherefore by their fruits ye shall know them.

means of grace for their greater fruitfulness might be duly administered. I then invited them to partake of the Holy Sacrament, and the rest of the congregation being Dissenters, after the prayer for the Church Militant, 45 remained to communicate. There were about 2 women or rather more so one man, and considering that the men generally were busy in the fishery, their number was not to be complained of.

After the Sacrament and service concluded, all the communicants came one by one to the rails of the altar to shake hands with me. None spoke, but tears stood in the eyes of many, and the shake of the hand was right hearty and affectionate. It appeared to me as or instead of the *osculum paci* [the Kiss of Peace], and I could almost think we had complied with the apostolic injunction "Salute one another" ἐν ἁγίῳ φιλήματι [*en hagioi philemati*].[20]

The men, women and children were well dressed in this cove and the men a remarkable, fine, athletic race. I was struck with the vast amount of black and mourning clothes in the congregation, and I found the cause to be the connection and relationship by marriage and descent of almost all the families in the settlement. Almost all the females in the congregation wore black bombazeen[21] gowns and black bonnets, and under the bonnets white caps, the men in general sailors' dress — the children in various clothes, not neatly done up about the hair but with fewer attempts at finery than I have noticed in some other settlements.

After the service, we measured the church, and Mr. Bridge took a drawing of the outside. Mr. Kingwell represented the desire of the people to have the church enlarged, and I promised to assist them in accomplishing the good work. It appears to me desirable to add about 15 feet to the east end of the church and a chancel of 6 or 7 feet beyond. After all concluded at the church, we adjourned to the cottage of a Mrs. Crane, who entertained us with excellent tea and bread and butter, pickled salmon and eggs. A most primitive and refreshing repast. Her husband was engaged in fishing, but the good lady represented in his and her own name and in that also of all their neighbours their need of a resident clergyman, begging me to supply one. I was much affected by the earnest manner of their petition, knowing what little hope there was of meeting their pious and reasonable wishes.

Leaving this settlement, in which I had been more interested than in any I had before visited, for many things had concurred to make me so: a lovely day, a novel and pleasant ride, a strange, picturesque settlement, a beautiful sea lying before me, presenting a succession of bays and promontories and studded with little boats known to be successfully employed in gathering God's bountiful gifts, reaping their yearly harvest (and we knew the interest attached to the work of the harvest in whatever country and of whatever kind), then the people well dressed and well behaved gathering about the neat wooden church, to which they were summoned by the two flags (their own and mine) on the staff — my extempore address, which appeared to

[20] 2 Corinthians, 13:12: Greet one another with an holy kiss.

[21] Bombazeen (also bombasine): a twill fabric constructed of a silk or rayon warp and worsted filling, often dyed black for mourning wear.

be apposite and successful — the devout attendance of the communicants and the primitive salutation at the conclusion of the service, with the earnest entreaties of my good and hospitable hostess for more regular and complete ministrations in their church and among them — all were exceedingly pleasant and painful.

I longed for dear friends from England, for their assistance and sympathy or even presence. Under such circumstances, I mean having them or any of them there with me. I do not know that I could have experienced or desired more unmixed or more full enjoyment. The sea seen through the windows of the church during the whole service, with the bold, bluff rocks projecting into it and the little boats scattered about it and all calm and bright and beautiful, continually caught my eye and deeply pleased and affected me.

We left this place about 2 o'clock and on our way to Bishop's Cove (formerly Bread and Cheese Cove), so christened by Bishop Spencer and distant from Island Cove only one mile. We visited the Newfoundland [School] Society's school placed on a rock about half way between the two settlements. The situation is convenient though rather exposed and highly picturesque, and this is the best I can say for it. The girls were generally pretty, well dressed and healthy in appearance; the boys in many instances had neither shoes nor stockings but otherwise were sufficiently clad. The master seems a simple, respectable man, young and inexperienced and half educated only — unmarried and lodging at Mr. Crane's house in Island Cove. This is one of the branch schools under the superintendence of Mr. Kingwell. A great number of half-grown girls chiefly of Bishop's Cove who from the Sunday School were assembled, who must, I should fear, under such controul be but little like scholars.

We reached Bishop's Cove church about 3 o'clock. The people did not generally assemble, as many of them had attended at Island Cove, and several were occupied in their boats. There is a tolerably neat and sufficient church here, but with the same Burtean arrangement and conglomeration of pulpit, reading desk, altar rails. The church is not painted, which the people appeared to regret, but I endeavoured to console them by assuring them I was quite satisfied. Here I was introduced to one of the little merchants who frequently take up their abode in these harbours and settlements and are too often great pests and the cause of great misery to the poor by supplying them with provisions till they get intolerably in debt and then getting possession of their houses and patches of land. This merchant at Bishop's Cove is named Gosse, and I heard no harm of him. We returned to Harbour Grace by nearly the same road as we had come by, reaching Mr. Ridley at ¼ before 6 o'clock. Some of the merchants and magistrates invited to meet me.

These two settlements together seem to deserve and require a resident priest who, with a deacon or deacons acting as schoolmasters and readers, might also have charge of Spaniard's Bay, the next settlement, about 4 miles off, now under the charge of Mr. [Joseph] Griffin, the deacon-schoolmaster resident there, who also officiates occasionally at New Harbour, 14 miles off in Trinity Bay. Island Cove

Church wants enlargement and of some fresh arrangement of pulpit. There are books for the desk and altar but no vessels, two fonts. The school requires much improvement.

The church at Bishop's Cove has no font, no books, no vessels and wants a fresh arrangement of pulpit &c.

Tuesday, July 30

Left my good host Mr. Ridley and Harbour Grace soon after 9 o'clock with Mr. Bridge on horseback for Spaniard's Bay, about 8 miles off. There resides Mr. [Joseph] Griffin, the deacon-schoolmaster, in the house of the Newfoundland School Society. There he keeps school, assisted by his wife. They are a simple couple, and he is very deaf, which would appear to disqualify him for the situation of schoolmaster! A great number of children were assembled of exceedingly wild, [uncottered] aspect, very indistinct in reading and speaking, which I attributed partly to the master's infirmity of deafness and his slow, thick pronunciation. The children of the first class read to me, but imperfectly and without any signs of intelligence, and their answers were innocent of any meaning in point.

There was a very perceptible difference between these people, in their dress and general appearance, and their neighbours at Island Cove. One reason given was from this place many families go to the Labrador during the fishing season and again some others into the woods in the winter, so that they are unsettled and in consequence untidy. They seem, however, of a different race or breed, and several of the children are [doighty] or nearly so. Probably also this is the oldest settlement, and the people have long intermarried with their relatives and neighbours.

Here the church is newly built and without a tower — not yet fitted up inside but prepared for galleries. A pulpit is erected in the centre, just before the altar, and the reading desk on the north side communicating with the pulpit by an arched staircase under which, Mr. Griffin remarked with much satisfaction, we could see the Communion! He asked me whether I should like a similar formation on the south side for the clerk, and there was to be [. . .] complete only without the [iron] — the pulpit being supported by a single log! Here I preached as yesterday without notes on St. John 14: 1-3[22] and afterwards administered the Holy Sacrament to 21 communicants, who took leave of us with the same primitive salutations. After the service, we partook of refreshment at Mr. Griffin's comfortable cottage and about 2 o'clock were put across the beautiful bay in a boat for Bay Roberts.

At Spaniard's Bay are no vessels, no font, no seats. The people seated themselves on logs and on benches brought from the schools. The books on the reading

[22]St. John 14: 1-3: Let not your heart be troubled: ye believe in God, believe also in me. In my Father's house are many mansions: if it were not so, I would have told you. I go to prepare a place for you. And if I go and prepare a place for you, I will come again, and receive you unto myself; that where I am, there ye may be also.

desk, which are handsome, are the gift of Lord Bexley,[23] who had very kindly furnished a bible and prayer book for each church where a schoolmaster has received orders. It would be very desirable to take upon myself the fitting up of this church to prevent the abominations of galleries and pews which are threatened and in preparation. In other respects, the church is neat — the pitch of the roof much the sharpest that I have seen and the carpenters' work the best done. The carpenter lives in the settlement and is a Roman Catholic.

Having crossed the beautiful bay and surmounted a ridge of land that forms the southern side of this bay and the northern side of Bay Roberts, we descended to Bay Roberts, where is a very long-struggling settlement. We proceeded along a very decent road upwards of a mile to the church, and on getting near it we perceived the parson, the Revd. Mr. Lowell,[24] who it appeared had been expecting us in the morning and had designed that his people should receive the Sacrament at my hands. As he is in priest's orders, there was not the same necessity for my administering it as in Spaniard's Bay and Island Cove.

He took us first to the schoolroom, where were assembled the children of the Sunday School whom he vaunted of as well instructed in the church Catechism, but they appeared far otherwise. He vaunted also of the numbers he had brought to the Sunday School, then of his having established a daily service in the afternoon in the church, besides regular services on saints' days. He next boasted of having obtained and fenced a burying ground, then of his great influence with his people, so that there would be no mistake. He is a genuine American — a young and unfortunately a single man, fancies himself a decided Churchman and, among other truly American ways of proving it, has named his dog "Chrysostom".[25] The dog was introduced to me as a son of the Church. Chryostom accompanied us to the church, of course, and when I remonstrated Mr. Lowell assured me he would not go beyond the vestry.

The service commenced at 6½ o'clock. Mr. Lowell said the prayers and, whether by way of intoning the service or for what other ecclesiastical object I know not, made such pauses between the sentences of the Confession that it was quite painful to hear him. The people kept coming in during the whole service, and the children were moving about, coming and going out in a degree that was almost

[23]Lord Bexley (1766-1851) was the younger son of Henry Vansittart, Governor of Bengal. An MP for 25 years, he had a reputation as a financial expert, and as Chancellor of the Exchequer for thirteen years left a surplus in spite of the costs of the Napoleonic wars. Offered a title in 1823, he spent his last years in charitable works, funding the building of churches and the distribution of bibles. He also helped found King's College London.

[24]Rev. Robert T. Lowell, who served in the period 1843-1847, was an American and a brother of the poet James Russell Lowell. The son of a Unitarian clergyman, born in Boston, he was educated at Harvard University and ordained a priest of the Episcopal Church in 1843. He is the author of *The New Priest in Conception Bay* (1858), the setting for which is Bay Roberts.

[25]John Chrysostom (349-c.407), whom the Orthodox Church and the Eastern Catholic Churches honor as a saint, was Archbishop of Constantinople.

intolerable. After Mr. Lowell's performance ended, I mounted the pulpit, which is in the centre just in front of a neat little chancel. There was the same moving and going to and fro — I had not proceeded far in my discourse when John Chrysostom marched deliberately up the church, as it might be supposed to enquire who was got into his, or his master's, place, but as it turned out to join his master at the altar! I stopped, of course, and insisted on his being thrown out, which his master, in great confusion, was obliged to perform. It is evidently a common practice, and I greatly fear that Mr. Lowell has another American gift, viz. that of lying. I spoke on St. John 14: 6.[26]

After the service, we adjourned to Mr. Lowell's lodgings, where he occupies two very tiny rooms, but he endeavoured to make us feel more comfortable and at ease by expatiating on the house he shortly intends to build — which is, he says, to be of stone and for which he has obtained a site. He gave us tea and bread and butter in abundance and some very nice scrods — which is the young cod — and was the first variety of the fish I have liked. The fishermen cook it better than professed artists. Here the American informed us of his powers and perfections, among other things equally wonderful that he was regularly descended from Magnus Troil.[27] He also recommended an Irish friend to me for orders.

As soon as tea was over, we motioned to depart for Port de Grave, but it appeared Mr. Lowell had provided no boat, and it struck me very forcibly that notwithstanding his great influence with his people, he did not like to ask for fear of being refused. However, we sallied forth and finding the N.S. schoolmaster stated our difficulty, which he presently relieved by applying to a Roman Catholic merchant who very readily and kindly put us across the bay. The moon was up and just before us, and the bay was like all the rest in fine weather, quite lovely — resembling pictures I have seen of Italian lakes covered with islands and divided by broken and low promontories and headlands. The ground about Bay Roberts is warmer and greener than in some other parts. The church is neat and substantial and seems to have all necessary furniture except the font. But between Chrysostom and his master, I fear, things are conducted in a loose way, or to say the least, in very bad taste.

We reached the next promontory or neck of land about 9 o'clock and found it the most sterile, forbidding rock we had yet encountered. The greater part of the settlement, or at least the town, is on the bare rock. Mr. [Johnstone] Vicars, the incumbent, was absent when we arrived at his house, and Mrs. Vicars upstairs ill — expecting her confinement [conclusion of pregnancy]. Mr. Vicars, however, returned before ten o'clock and welcomed us very friendly. Mr. Vicars is a connection and friend of Mr. Moore, my old master at Rugby, and his father is a clergyman, for many years resident in Exeter but now holding a small living in Dorsetshire. His

[26]St. John 14: 6: Jesus saith unto him, I am the way, the truth, and the life: no man cometh unto the Father, but by me.

[27]Magnus Troil: a character in *The Pirate* (1822), by Sir Walter Scott.

lady is the daughter of Mr. Garrett of St. John's, the sheriff. His house is rented of a Mr. Pinsent of Harbour Grace and is small. Mr. Vicars has two settlements and churches in his mission near to each other about 3 miles, Port de Grave and Bareneed.

Wednesday, July 31

We walked to Bareneed along rocks bare indeed about 11 o'clock through a thick fog. Bareneed is a fishing settlement like the rest, with its stages and flakes projecting into or hanging over the sea or occasionally running into the land. The stage is nearest to the water, generally on a jutting rock and is a covered shed with a door opening to the sea. Here the fish are received from the boats, being pitched up with a long stick having a fork or spike at the end. In this stage the fish are sorted and split and thence carried to the flake, which is slightly made and supported on tall wooden legs very straggling and adapted to the rock or shore on which they stand. On these the flakes are laid and covered with boughs on which the fish are laid out to dry. This is the character of them all, and the whole frontage of a settlement is frequently occupied by them, and advantage is taken of every ledge and jutting rock to erect a stage or flakes, which at this time were everywhere covered with the produce of the deep sea — as the fields in England with hay or corn. After lying to dry and for that purpose being turned frequently, they are put up on round rocks, which are covered with bark, and the fish is then said to be "made".

Bareneed about the church is the most crowded and irregular settlement I have yet seen. The church is small and crowded with galleries and pews of the worst description. The tower is on the south side and forms the entrance and porch, and the pulpit and reading desk and altar, on the Burtean principle, are immediately opposite the entrance. There was very good attendance, and after the prayers I addressed the people on I Corinthians 4:1-5.[28]

The master of the school is a young man of Port de Grave, of small attainments but apparently amiable. His scholars did not shew any proficiency — they were generally well dressed but shewed signs of disease either from bad living or intermarriage which I had not observed before.

On walking back, a place was pointed out half way between Bareneed and Port de Grave where several Englishmen were once massacred by natives. The origin of

[28]I Corinthians 4: 1-5: Let a man so account of us, as of the ministers of Christ, and stewards of the mysteries of God. Moreover it is required in stewards, that a man be found faithful. But with me it is a very small thing that I should be judged of you, or of man's judgement: yea, I judge not mine own self. For I know nothing by myself; yet am I not hereby justified: but he that judgeth me is the Lord. Therefore judge nothing before the time, until the Lord come, who both will bring to light the hidden things of darkness, and will make manifest the counsels of the hearts: and then shall every man have praise of God.

the name Port de Grave is not exactly known,[29] but it is generally supposed to indicate the sad and sombre appearance of the rocks as you approach them from the sea and enter the harbour. If the name were English, Port of the Graves, the meaning might well be derived from the number of burying places in the settlement, of which there are 8 or 10 in different parts, generally marked out by large stones from England and enclosed by a wooden rails. It was the custom, before the churchyards were consecrated, to bury in gardens, or by the roadsides or any place as convenience or fancy might point out, and the clergyman has more than once got into disgrace by refusing to bury in these private and unconsecrated cemeteries.

At Port de Grave, the fish flakes and stages are carried out to neighbouring rocks in a very ingenious way, and I requested Mr. Bridge to take drawings of two or three. The church is Burtean and full of pews and galleries and not affording room enough for the people. A new church seems required, for there is no possibility of making additions to or otherwise enlarging the present one.

I preached a written old discourse which I had preached before at Harbour Grace: St. Matthew 5:20.[30] The singing was better at Bareneed and here at Port de Grave than usual. At Bay Roberts, chaunting was attempted with distinguished success. After service we found Mrs. Vicars waiting for us and preparing tea. She seems a sensible, amiable woman and very near her confinement. I was much pleased with Mr. Vicars — he is quiet, sensible, gentlemanly and pious, a most pleasing contrast to his vaunting, vivacious neighbour. Said neighbour called today at Mr. Vicars's and not finding me at home left a note in Latin for me, the joint composition probably of himself and Chrysostom, as it was a decided specimen of Dog Latin.

I am inclined to think Mr. Vicars could do very well for Harbour Grace, but it is a pity to move him from a place where he is so usefully employed.

Thursday, August 1

Soon after 9 o'clock, we were started on a boat through the fog towards Salmon Cove, which we reached about 10½ o'clock coasting near Bareneed, which looked interesting looming through the fog. On the wharf or stage at Salmon Cove I found the Revd. Mr. Martine, the missionary, and Mr. Greene, the magistrate and Collector of Customs, and hoped that their juxtaposition indicated a reconciliation, but alas! not so — they were still at enmity and did not speak to each other, tho' each spoke to me.

There is only a chapel/schoolhouse here, licensed by the late Bishop, the property of the N.S. Society. The schoolmaster, Mr. Ryall, lives nearby, and his wife had

[29]Port de Grave was first inhabited by the French, who used the beaches or *graves* for drying their fish.

[30]St. Matthew 5: 20: For I say unto you, That except your righteousness shall exceed the righteousness of the scribes and Pharisees, ye shall in no case enter into the kingdom of heaven.

just been confined. In his house I saw a bake pot in operation, which is in an iron pot closely covered with an iron lid which is again covered with [embers]. In this, hanging over the fire like a kettle, small loaves of bread and other matters are nicely baked. This is the common way of baking in the fishermen's house, but biscuit is more commonly used, which is bought by the bag at St. John's.

In the schoolroom, we had the morning service, and I preached on St. John 15: 1-5.[31] Very attentive poor people who waited about the door and seemed disappointed that they had not an opportunity of shaking me by the hand. I remained a time to examine the children and concluded from their performance that their master (Mr. Ryall) may be more skilful as a carpenter (which he is by trade) than as a teacher. After the service, Mr. Martine drove me in his little waggon towards Brigus, and on my way I called on Mr. Greene, his enemy, and desired him, if he still wished to bring any charge against Mr. Martine, to attend at the school at 5 o'clock this evening.

Arriving at Brigus about 2 o'clock, we visited the church, which is not yet quite completed, tho' nearly; all but the tower is done, and it appears well done. It is fitted up just like St. Thomas's, except that there is no recess for the altar, nor gallery about or behind it. The pews are constructed with a board going down from the front of each seat to the ground, so that it is really impossible to kneel. The walls of the church are plastered and the cieling of the roof and the underside of the galleries. There is also a little shabby stained glass in the east window and a bell in the tower, and the windows and tower are more ornamental than usual. There is no font and no Communion plate. The pulpit and reading desk might easily be moved with advantage.

At 3 we dined. Mr. And Mrs. Martine are both Scotch. He was educated at Edinburgh but took no degree. They have no children. He appears a man of most unhappy temper, prying, prating, quarrelsome (and, appears worse than all, false). I heartily wish he were provided for elsewhere. I met Mr. Greene according to appointment at 5 o'clock, taking with me Mr. Martine to hear the charges which might be made against him, Mr. Bridge as witness. After some difficulty and disputation, I prevailed with Mr. Martine to offer his hand to Mr. Greene, which the latter, with a very bad grace, accepted, evidently disappointed that he had not an opportunity of uttering his complaints and accusations. He, like his antagonist, is a hotheaded, ill-conditioned man, but, I fear, has the best [not] in respect of honesty and the chief cause of complaint. I fear the reconciliation is not likely to be very real or permanent, but I could do no more.

[31]St. John 15: 1-5: I am the true vine, and my Father is the husbandman. Every branch in me that beareth not fruit he taketh away: and every branch that beareth fruit, he purgeth it, that it may bring forth more fruit. Now ye are clean through the word which I have spoken unto you. Abide in me, and I in you. As the branch cannot bear fruit of itself, except it abide in the vine; no more can ye, except ye abide in me. I am the vine, ye are the branches: He that abideth in me, and I in him, the same bringeth forth much fruit: for without me ye can do nothing.

At 6½ o'clock, we went to the church, where a tolerable congregation was gathered, and I preached on Hebrews 4:16[32] (an old discourse), part of the Second Lesson of this evening's service. The singing was loud and discordant.

Brigus is a place very noted for success in the seal fishery, and many of the inhabitants are considered wealthy. It was formerly a place of considerable trade, but a wealthy merchant nearly monopolized the whole and then broke. He is now a stipendiary magistrate in the place and a Dissenter. The Methodists have a large meeting house here, close to the church. There is also a nice Roman Catholic chapel. The priest has a good house and farm near adjoining the town. There is the same aspect of barrenness here as in other places. Salmon Cove has more plain and pleasant land than any settlement I have seen, and I hope, if it please God, to see it still more pleasant when a decent church looks upon the plain and bay. Brigus be gone!

The kalmias between Salmon Cove and Brigus are numerous and beautiful [. . .].

Friday, August 2

After resting at Mr. Martine's, I started at 9 o'clock with Mr. Bridge and Frederic in the packet for Portugal Cove, en route for St. John's. We visited in going down to the wharf the Newfoundland Society school, of which Mr. Mills is the master. He also is in enmity with Mr. Martine and appeared quite disposed to enter the lists with him in the way of accusation and complaint. The room is the largest and best I have seen, and the house is neat and comfortable. Mr. Bridge slept there. We left the pier about half past nine or a quarter to ten o'clock, a bright, clear, warm day but unfortunately with no wind, and in consequence we did not reach the cove till quite late evening: 8½ o'clock.

We passed close to Belle Isle [Bell Island] and saw a very pretty settlement called Lance Cove, which reminded me much of some little Devonshire valleys. The land appears good and rapidly getting under cultivation. A church is built, but no clergyman attends it and, I fear, there is no prospect of one. Here resides our friend Mr. Pitts, who offers to give a piece of land for a burying ground at Portugal Cove. I should like to live by him.

I took advantage of our long voyage to write up my journal to this place. *Gratias dio*. [Thanks be to God.] My impression, on the whole, with respect to the Church is that if she had means and ministers, she might at this time strike some deep roots in these localities. At the same time, we want ministers of prudence and piety — Englishmen, not Scotch or American. Learning is not requisite, for neither Romanists or Dissenters make pretence to any. I do not perceive the need at present of more ministers to reside in the different settlements but should prefer having 3 at

[32]Hebrews 4: 16: Let us therefore come boldly unto the throne of grace, that we may obtain mercy, and find grace to help in time of need.

Harbour Grace who might go more frequently and regularly to the out-harbours but reside together in once place. So at Brigus there should be two at least.

There is great want of all church furniture, and especially of fonts, and much money is required for altering and fitting up ill-managed and unfinished churches and to prevent the selling and letting of pews. The pulpits generally should be taken down and the space about the altar enlarged, opened and beautified. Better arrangements, of a more systematic kind, should be made for collecting money, or payments in fish, and the people should be exhorted to give a tenth of their income to Church purposes. The clergy whom I have visited all seem anxious about their churches and congregations and industrious, but the Americans and Scotchmen are very unsatisfactory, and the latter, I fear, is doing primitive mischief. The people at Harbour Grace are calculating, cold, and I fear indifferent about religion, though not indifferent about all the forms of religion. They have been spoilt, and unless they can have a minister they like will, I fear, be discontented and troublesome for a time till they are better taught. Methodists are powerful at Carbonear. The others are a simpleminded people generally and may continue so and improve if not ruined by [pews]. Brigus is quite unsettled.

The temperance principles are reported to have done much good, and I have reason to hope and believe that morality is much increased and that the people generally are at least as chaste, honest, and temperate and [moralistic] as in the villages of England. They are also not unkind or uncharitable, and the different sects have very little animosity or dispute. I always except Brigus. The Romanists generally are very quiet and respectful, and the Methodists are not particularly evil-minded. They both feel that the Church [of England] occupies an honourable place and are inclined still more to respect her, as she respects herself.

The Newfoundland School Society's teachers are generally respectable and amiable men and doing good by their example and influence with the people — but as teachers they are very inefficient and unsatisfactory. Their schools are wretchedly found in books and of a very dubious, heretical character. The deacon schoolmasters are much taken away from their schools, I fear, by their [first] avocation. I did not see one school that appeared in a satisfactory state in any respect, and I fear if the Dissenters should set up schools near any of these they would easily lead away the children. They are certainly taught nothing in these schools to make them understand or love the Church or to make them "know them that labour among them and are over them in the Lord and admonish them and to esteem very highly in love for their work's sake".[33] I perceive also that the clergyman does not visit or otherwise direct these schools, having no authority to interfere. There is no Sunday School connected with this Society, and the Church Catechism is not taught on the weekdays.

[33] 1 Thessalonians: 5: 12-13: And we beseech you, brethren, to know them which labour among you, and are over you in the Lord, and admonish you; And to esteem them very highly in love for their work's sake. And be at peace among yourselves.

The Protestant boards of education are likely, I fear, to cause much evil and eventually strife if they last — but as they contain in themselves the elements of confusion, so, I would hope, of dissolution. God grant me wisdom to pilot our little ship safely through these rocks and shoals for Christ's sake. Amen.

Saturday, August 3

Said the prayers in St. Thomas's Church at 9 o'clock. Directly after the service received letters from England by the steamer *North America*. Occupied the rest of the day in reading and digesting the news — chewing the cud of sweet and bitter fancies. Dined at Government House and met a Capt. Bayfield of the ship *Fulmar*e and Mr. Haviland of Prince Edward Island, very nice men apparently.

Sunday, August 4

Went at 10 o'clock to St. John's Sunday School. Boys and girls in the same room. Teachers respectable persons of the town, Messrs. Wilson, Wood and Trunningham &c with the boys. I took the first class of boys, who read generally pretty well, and answered questions about the feasts of the Jewish and Christian church indifferently and said the Catechism badly. Nice boys apparently and pretty well ordered. A deficiency of books.

I preached and assisted in administering the Sacrament at St. John's Church — 115 communicants. I preached in the afternoon at St. Thomas's Church. Palairet went to Petty Harbour.

Monday, August 5

Prayers at St. Thomas's at 9½ o'clock. Mr. Blackman officiated. Occupied the whole day in writing letters. Palairet dined at Government House.

Tuesday, August 6

Palairet said the prayers at St. Thomas's Church. Sent off my letters by the steamer *North America*. Unpacked furniture, books &c. Received an application from Mr. [Augustus] Bayly for a nomination for his son to the [Theological] Institution. Dined with Mr. Bridge at 6 o'clock and met Mr. Dunscombe and several ladies.

Wednesday, August 7

Wrote a long letter to the Revd. Mr. [William] Scott about wooden churches and other ecclesiastical purposes and proceedings.[34]. At 4 o'clock the Governor em-

[34]See Appendix A.

barked on board the *Eurydice* frigate (Capt. Elliott), intending to proceed on an excursion round the island, but there being no wind he returned almost immediately. At half past ten o'clock he again embarked and slept on board, taking with him his aide-de-camp, Lieut. Harvey, and secretary, Mr. Crowdy. I take up my abode at Bishop's Court, having taken leave of my kind, hospitable and agreeable hosts Sir John and Lady Harvey, by whom I have now been entertained more than a month, that is from the day of my landing July 4 to the present time, August 7. God bless and recompense them.

3. Sir John and Lady Harvey

Sir John Harvey (a major-general and K.C.B. and K.C.H. &c) is the son of an English clergyman and appears to have entered the army at an early age. He served with credit in Egypt, India and America. He commanded (as colonel) in the Battle of Lundy's Lane,[1] where he was opposed to General [Winfield] Scott, to whom he was personally known and who commanded his men (rifles) not to hurt Col. Harvey but to take him alive. Fortunately, after 6 hours hard fighting, the Americans were repulsed. Sir John being a Whig and having some powerful friends (Marquis of Anglesea[2] and others) and personally known to William IV was appointed to some places of civil and diplomatic trust.

By the Whigs he was made Lieutenant-Governor of Prince Edward Island and afterwards Lieutenant-Governor of New Brunswick. That post he occupied when the Whigs went out of office, but not being of very stiff political principles and requiring the emoluments of his place he gladly accepted the permission to continue his government. Unfortunately, he gave offence to Lord Sydenham[3] by some ill-considered or unauthorized negotiations on the boundary question, into which it appears he was led by his old friend and enemy Gen. Scott. Lord Sydenham considered himself in some way compromised or interfered with and required Sir John's removal from New Brunswick. He was thereupon appointed to succeed Capt. Prescott[4] in the Government of Newfoundland in the year 1840 and arrived at St. John's for that purpose.

[1]The Battle of Lundy's Lane, 25 July 1814, was the bloodiest and most tenaciously fought battle of the War of 1812. British and Canadian forces stood on the battlefield at Lundy's Lane, the present-day Niagara Falls, Ont., to repel an invasion by U.S. forces, effectively ending America's attempt to invade Canada.

[2]Henry Paget, 2nd Earl of Uxbridge and Marquess of Anglesey (1768-1854), began his career in the infantry but entered the cavalry. He commanded with distinction the cavalry and horse artillery at Waterloo.

[3]Charles Poulett Thomson, 1st Baron Sydenham (1799-1841), first Governor of the united Province of Canada.

[4]Henry Prescott (1783-1874), Governor of Newfoundland from 1834, submitted his resignation in January 1839, but it was not accepted. Thus, he stayed on for another two years and resigned a second time in May 1841, then returned to naval life.

He is spoken of as a gallant and good officer. As far as I can judge, he is a man of talent and education but with more knowledge of men and manners than of books. Having moved much in various societies and visited so many quarters of the globe and mixed in so many affairs of military and civil service, he has acquired much information and knows events of much historical interest. His conversation is agreeable but whether from having risen from a comparatively humble origin or not having completed his education before entering into active service, it too often turns upon his own projects and performances and his connection or acquaintance with great men, as Lord Anglesey, the Duke of Richmond[5], his dear friend William IV &c. He is also a little over-polite and makes rather too large professions of regard and benevolence. In his government, he appears to attempt to please all parties, partly, I think, from a desire to be popular, partly hoping to reconcile differences and make the wheels of government move easily, if not harmoniously, and partly from real good nature and kindness of heart which does not know how to refuse or disoblige.

His theory of government is that of his great master, the Duke, present expediency or what the apparent necessity of the case requires (to gain a battle or take a town or do what is to be done) without any regard to fixed principles or the eternal fitness of things. By birth, education and preference, he is a Churchman and has a pleasure in the services of the Church, and for a soldier and diplomatist has religious feelings and tendencies, but alas! even here there is little fixed, real and definite. If the majority should prefer any other form of religion, or none, they must be indulged or allowed — and so it is, I suppose, of all diplomatists and politicians. God is not in all their thoughts — I mean as diplomatists or politicians — though as private persons He may be. It is very sad, very awful that government cannot be conducted on Christian principles and, I suppose, not on any if not on these.

Sir John as a governor is really desirous to promote the interests (according to his views) of the colony and gives both his time and pains. He has turned attention with good effect to agriculture and the improvement of roads and negotiates with the French for the occupation of part of the island now ceded to them [the French Shore], so far at least that no English can lawfully settle there. His great object, and a wise one, is to settle the island. His great defect as a governor lies in his desire to please and be popular and his inability or unwillingness to refuse any request, and the issue seems likely to be that of the fable that seeking to please everybody he will please nobody, I mean as a governor.[6] As a gentleman, his urbanity, hospitality and real kindness cannot fail to please, and I should hope all who have experienced these at his hands will be ready to declare themselves obliged to shew themselves grateful, as I desire to do.

[5]Charles Henry Gordon-Lennox, 6th Duke of Richmond (1818-1903), served in the Royal Horse Guards and was aide-de-camp to the Duke of Wellington.

[6]See Aesop's Fables : "The Man and His Two Sweethearts."

Lady Harvey is the daughter of Lord Lake,[7] a very amiable, hospitable, excellent person, having all her feelings and desires good and kind, disliking ostentation and parade and sincerely wishing to lead a quiet and peaceable life in all godliness and honesty — but being a soldier's daughter and a soldier's wife, she has not had her attention turned to devotion or religious study. She is delicate in bodily health and not strong in mind, but sensible and judicious with a just insight into character. Both Sir John and Lady Harvey cordially approve of the daily morning service in the church and, wind or weather permitting, regularly attend it.

The only members of the family now at home are Mr. Henry Harvey, who acts as his father's private secretary, and Warwick Harvey, a lieutenant and his father's aide-de-camp. Mr. Henry Harvey appears a well disposed, amiable and sensible person but is remarkably taciturn and reserved. He is married to Ella Spencer, eldest daughter of the Bishop of Jamaica, my predecessor. She is thought of [as] fancy, thinks herself pretty. I think her (but hope I may be mistaken) indolent, selfish and proud. They have one little girl a year old who is a nice child and much prized by her grandparents (Sir J. and Lady H.) but is scarcely noticed by father or mother. Lieut. Harvey is pleasant (though quiet) and very gentlemanly in his manners, apparently fond of gaiety and athletic sports, hunting, driving and, *sicut est mos* [as the habit is], of young men and young soldiers.

[7]Gerard Lake, 1st Viscount Lake (1744-1808), British general.

4. St. John's

Visits to Broad Cove, Bell Island, Portugal Cove and Pouch Cove

Thursday, August 8

After a good sleep on my own mattress in Bishop's Court, I saw at ½ past six in the morning the *Eurydice* sailing slowly and majestically down the harbour, carrying our *Caesar eiusque fortunas*.[1] It was nearly or full an hour before she had cleared the Narrows: a light wind and beautiful day. I made some calls with Mr. Bridge and dined at 3 o'clock under the auspices of Dean Palairet. At 8 o'clock we took a pleasant promenade in front of Government House. Prayers at 9 o'clock. Unpacked and arranged all my personal linen.

Friday, August 9

Said the prayers in St. Thomas's Church — had a visit from the Attorney General, acting Chief Justice Simms.[2] Went with Mr. Blackman and Palairet to examine the upper chambers of St. Thomas's Church, decided on making the room formerly used for a Sunday School a Registrar's Office, propounded to Palairet my plan of a school and found him compliant and implacable. Drew out a plan or prospectus of the same. Went to the parish church and submitted the prospectus to Mr. Bridge.

Saturday, August 10

Submitted the prospectus to Mr. Blackman and after revision to the Attorney General (Mr. James Simms). Both approved, and the latter promises to send two sons

[1] *Caesar eiusque fortunas*: Caesar and his fortunes. This is likely a facetious reference to Caesar's sea crossing in an open boat. When the steersman decided to turn back in poor weather, Caesar reproached him and said, according to Plutarch, "Go on, my friend, and fear nothing; you carry Caesar and his fortune in your boat." See *Plutarch's Lives*, 2: 225.

[2] James A. Simms (1779-1863), appointed Attorney General in 1828, was an early opponent of representative government.

and to give the concern all the support in his power. He appears amiable and hearty and withal is a man of judgment and long experience in colonial affairs.

Sunday, August 11

Palairet went to Torbay, accompanied by Mr. Lightbourn. At 9½ o'clock, I went to the St. Thomas's Sunday School, found a few children assembled but no master or teacher except one of the young men from the [Theological] Institution. After waiting a few minutes and no one appearing, I read one of Bishop Blomfield's prayers, being informed by the student that was the form commonly used, though it did not appear to me that the book was easily found or had ever before been used. Soon after I had finished came Miss Frampton (Mr. Spearman's sister), who manages, it is said, for Mrs. Blackman in her absence. Then another of the students and a Miss Carrington and soon after the children of the regimental school with their master (the sergeant) and his wife the mistress. These manage and teach in the daily regimental school at Signal Hill and appear sensible, careful people according to their means and knowledge. The numbers were about 40 girls and 30 boys. The lessons appeared to be just what each chose to learn. All (of the upper classes) seemed to know the collect for the day, and most also learned an explanation and instruction on the same from a little Catechism composed by Mr. Wix — but some learnt Scripture, some hymns (of various sorts), some catechisms, and these in the same class, so that nearly the whole time was consumed in these miscellaneous performances — and very little done in reading or repeating the church catechism. I remained till half past ten o'clock, and Mr. Blackman did not make his appearance. The children were not properly arranged nor in such good order as at St. John's.

At eleven I went to St. Thomas's Church, where I preached. At two o'clock I went to the Government House and took luncheon with Lady Harvey. At 3 to St. Thomas's Church a second time when Mr. Blackman preached one of his unreal, pompous, flowery discourses, pleasing for aught I know to colonial ears polite, but to mine most painful. It gave to the whole service an unreal, unmeaning character, which made me very sad and sick at heart. Palairet returned about half past 5 o'clock, not well pleased with his congregation. At six and half o'clock I went to St. John's Church for Mr. Bridge's sake that he might not preach himself to death in giving life to his people. I preached in his theatre, which was lighted up and well frequented, boxes, galleries and all. Anything but a church.

Monday, August 12

Occupied after prayers in unpacking books &c. Mr. Pall, one of the students, read the lessons in the church. Received a visit from Mr. and Mrs. Ridley, Mr. Robinson, Mr. Green, Mr. G.H. Emerson. Called on Mr. and Mrs. Thomas. Dined at 5 o'clock.

Received a present of a marble vase with flowers from Mr. Heathcote. Walked with Palairet towards the "Billies"[3] but not far enough to reach them.

Tuesday, August 13

Unpacking and arranging furniture nearly the whole day. Called on Lady Harvey, Mrs. Law and Mrs. Heathcote, Mrs. Saunders &c. In the evening, after dinner, walked to Kitty Vitty [Quidi Vidi], calling on Mrs. Bennett, where I saw a Mrs. Prowse and another but not Miss Shepherd.

Wednesday, August 14

Finished unpacking my books. Called with Palairet on Mr. H. Thomas, Mrs. Spearman and Major Robe. At 7 o'clock in the evening I attended the meeting of the Church Society in the room of Newfoundland Schoolhouse and gave them an account of my visit to Conception Bay.

Thursday, August 15

Started at 8½ o'clock with Palairet, Mr. Bridge in Mr. Bridge's carriage for Broad Cove; went along the road leading to Portugal Cove about 7 miles and then walked through the woods about 5 miles to Broad Cove. The road has only lately been cleared of trees and has not yet been levelled or otherwise made. It is consequently very stony and uneven, and there are many slight bogs or swamps. We passed two or three picturesque ponds, but no cleared land appeared till we came near and over Broad Cove, when from a cleared spot on the top of a hill we had a beautiful view of the bay and of the islands lying in it, with the distant headlands of Harbour Grace, Brigus, &c. On the top of this hill, two or three of the inhabitants met us, and the Bishop and his chaplains must have presented to their eyes a somewhat strange appearance, each carrying his coat on his arm and having the bare sleeves, but as our friends appeared in the same dress or undress, they, I dare say, conceived us attired *selon les règles* [according to the rules]. However, they were very hearty and respectful in their greetings and salutations, and after resting a short time at the cottage of one named Symms, a man supporting his own family, his aged mother, his widowed sister with 3 children, we proceeded to the church. There many of the inhabitants were assembled who represented to us their desire to proceed with their church but inability for want of funds.

It is not yet finished, even externally, being only clapboarded up half the walls. The thickness of the frame I found to be only 4 inches. I urged the people to exert themselves, and one man promised for himself and proposed to his neighbours to

[3]"The Billies": home of Dr. William Carson, situated on what is now Rostellan St., near Rennies River. See Paul O'Neill, *The Oldest City*, 1: 286-7.

give each man two quintals of fish, which was generally agreed to, but some were reported as defaulters — and this seemed to throw a damp on the spirits or exertions of others. The church is nicely situated on a hill with a very picturesque and extensive churchyard sloping down nearly to the sea. The people are a simple, obliging race, earnestly desirous to have a clergyman among them.

After much conversation and exhortation with and to them to persevere in faith and patience, we left the place in a boat rowed by 8 of the inhabitants of the cove for the beautiful little settlement of Lance Cove on Bell Isle [Bell Island]. This cove much resembles some of the little combes or coves on the Devonshire coast or on the Isle of Wight, and the island itself may be looked upon as the Isle of Wight of the colony. It is much more fertile than the neighbouring coast of Newfoundland and has nearly the same red soil and appearance, with trees growing down to the very edge of the water, which we notice on the south coast of Devon. There is also a nice beach of a mile long extending nearly from Lance Cove to Bell Isle beach, the only two settlements on the island.

The former is chiefly occupied by members of our church and the latter almost exclusively by Romanists. At Lance Cove resides Mr. Pitts, who is mentioned in my journal (July 27th) as presenting the church at Portugal Cove with a piece of land for a burying place and intending to furnish a pulpit of cedar of Lebanon for the little church at Lance Cove. This church has been built upon land given by Mr. Pitts, a very beautiful and convenient locality and close to his own little farm. It is like that of Broad Cove, of ample dimensions. The church is only finished externally and the walls inside neglected, but there is only a single floor, which, as ground circulates freely beneath, will be very cold. Our crew from Broad Cove accompanied us to the church, but through some blunder the inhabitants of the island had not been made aware of our intended visit, and only a few came together to make us welcome and offer us civilities. We sat down on the ground in the churchyard to partake of our bread and cheese and biscuits, which we had brought with us, and seldom have I so much enjoyed any repast.

The day was fair, calm and bright, the ground (our carpet and table) was soft, warm and clean; our journey and exercise had been long and heavy enough to create a good appetite, and we were engaged, as we hoped, in a proper and profitable and pious work. Before us lay the beautiful blue sea, just buffeted by a wind, which promised us a quick and pleasant sail homewards, and looking across the bay we saw the coast of Newfoundland and the cove we had just visited with so much interest and satisfaction. In the churchyard itself was the little church of wood on our left hand, and near it our stout, honest crew partaking of the viands which we had provided and faring as ourselves.

There are some pretty groups of trees, rather an unusual feature, remaining in the churchyard, and the slope of the ground towards the sea is pleasant. Immediately around the churchyard are fine meadows from which the grass had just, in some cases, been cut, and was making into hay, and among these the white houses of the settlers, and in front of the whole the picturesque fish stages and flakes well covered with their sea harvest. At our back and right hand or western side were lofty hills covered to the summit with the fir and spruce and showing great luxuriance of growth and a pleasing variety of outline.

Mr. Bridge took a sketch of these hills and also of the church, and while he was so engaged, a very nicely dressed and well behaved woman came to offer the hospitalities of her house. These we were obliged to decline for want of time and merely adjourned to the house of Mr. Pitts to ask for a little water and milk, for we were not provided with any potables. Our wants were quickly and cheerfully supplied, and after visiting the school, which is one established by the Board of Education on the schoolmaster, a Presbyterian, we took our departure from this fair rock.

The wind fulfilled its promises, and we had a delightful sail to Portugal Cove, reaching it in about an hour and twenty minutes. Here we found Mr. Bridge's carriage ready and prepared for us, and after taking leave of my crew and promising (God willing) to give them service and a sacrament at Portugal Cove next Sunday, we departed about 5 o'clock and reached St. John's at 6½ o'clock, having had a most pleasant and prosperous day.

Friday, August 16

Today a regatta, a boat race at Quidi Vidi Pond, when a kind of fair is held on the banks in tents and booths erected for this occasion. In a quarrel in one of the booths a young man was killed by a stone thrown by a woman which struck him on the left breast. I attended a vestry meeting at St. John's Church at which it was agreed and ordered that the place of the pulpit should be altered and the singers brought down from the gallery and put at the east end of the church. Spent a considerable time in the church, pointing out and requiring other alterations in the pews for the accommodation of more families. Attended the service at 7 o'clock when Palairet said the prayers and Mr. Bridge preached.

Saturday, August 17

Engaged greatest part of the day in writing letters for the next mail to England. At 12 o'clock went to meet the carpenter at St. John's Church to give directions about the projected alterations. Poor Mr. Bridge in a tease about the opposition of a Mr. Gregory, who does not consent to have his pew touched. Gregory the Great,[4] I presume.

[4]St. Gregory the Great or Pope Gregory I (c. 540-604) was Pope from 590 until his death.

Sunday, August 18

Went with Palairet in Mr. Bridge's carriage to Portugal Cove. Left St. John's 5 minutes before nine and reached the cove half past ten o'clock. Ready to meet us first was [the] sexton, some quarter of a mile out of the cove, and then the schoolmaster near his staff. I went into the school and heard the first class read and say the Church Catechism. Reading very imperfect — Catechism repeated pretty decently — and other lessons learnt.

Went to the church at 11 o'clock: found a good congregation, chiefly Broad Cove people, assembled. Palairet baptized 4 children, three from Broad Cove, one from Lance Cove. I preached, and we administered the Holy Communion to 17 communicants, chiefly inhabitants of Broad Cove. The service was not over till nearly two o'clock.. We retired to the master's cottage and ate our frugal meal of sandwiches, or rather I ate them and Palairet looked on and took a biscuit. Had an afternoon service when Palairet preached. The people behaved pretty well at both services, but the great gallery promotes spitting and other irreverence. The women sat on one side of the church and the men on the other (north). At the time of receiving, the communicants all came together and knelt before the altar as near as they could, though few of course comparatively could be at the rails. The rest were close touching them behind. After the celebration of the Communion, the communicants all came to the rails to shake hands with me.

We left the cove at 4½ o'clock and reached St. John's at 6 o'clock, and I drove down immediately to the parish church, where I preached the same sermon as I had done at the cove. Church not so full as last Sunday on account of the rain.

Monday, August 19

Expecting the steamer with letters a great part of the day. Gave directions to a carpenter about some alterations at St. Thomas's Church for the accommodation of books. Called on Lady Harvey and Mr. Green and others.

Tuesday, August 20

Mr. Earle, the organist, attended to give a lesson to the theological students in singing. Engaged him to attend 3 times a week, Tuesdays, Thursdays and Saturdays. Gave further directions to the carpenter.

Wednesday, August 21

North America arrived from Halifax, bringing many letters from dear friends in England. Employed nearly the whole of the day reading, learning and inwardly digesting[5] their contents. Called with Mr. Bridge on the Messrs. Dickenson, clerks to Mr. Thomas and friends of Mr. Macken's family. Also on Messrs. Wagnell and Wilson, Mr. Hutchings, Lieut. Carter and others. Received my small seal or ring from Halifax. Called on Lady Harvey.

Thursday, August 22

Engaged the whole day after prayers and [. . .] lesson in writing letters — a very wet day. Received notice of the arrival of the *Martha Harrison* at Harbour Grace with my goods: a small box, a paper parcel, a picture of Mr. Eden's church and a letter were forwarded by carrier and other things reported safe.

Friday, August 23

Said the prayers at St. Thomas's Church. Saw the departure of the troops (artillery) from the barracks to embark on board the *Apollo* for Quebec and the entry of the other troops sent from England in the *Apollo* to take their place. One generation passeth away and another cometh.[6] The same band that played one party out played the other in.

Wrote letters the whole day till evening prayers, when I went to St. John's Church.

Saturday, August 24, St. Bartholomew

Sent off my letters. Went to St. John's Church at 11 o'clock. Baptized a child — the daughter of the N.F. schoolmaster in the church after the Second Lesson — the first child I have baptized in Newfoundland. Walked with Palairet at 4 o'clock. Received my packages from Liverpool per *Martha Harrison*.

Sunday, August 25

Went to St. Thomas's Sunday School, found the attendance larger and Miss Frampton labouring to produce improvements. Mr. Blackmore came not. Preached in St. Thomas's Church. A large congregation. Went at two o'clock to Government House, where I made a dinner of luncheon. Only Lady Harvey, Mr. And Mrs. Harvey at home. Went at 3 o'clock to St. John's, where I preached the same sermon

[5]An allusion to the Collect for the Second Sunday in Advent, which begins, "Blessed Lord, who hast caused all holy Scriptures to be written for our learning; Grant that we may in such wise hear them read, mark, learn, and inwardly digest them . . . ."

[6]Ecclesiastes 1: 4: One generation passeth away, and another generation cometh: but the earth abideth for ever.

as in the morning at St. Thomas's — a small congregation, chiefly of poor people and servants.

A funeral after the service which I witnessed. I used to think it would not matter where one's body was laid, but really I do not know how it would be possible to rest in such a dismal, dirty, desolate graveyard as this. O how I sighed for a view of dear Bicknor's nice walks and walls. Here the fence is of miserable boards, broken and dirty — no walk through or into the churchyard, plenty of iron rails and other fences round the graves, lofty stones and tombs of the most offensive kind, and rocks of a great size thrown about everywhere. Palairet, who went to Petty Harbour, returned about 8 o'clock well pleased with his day's walk and duty and a conversation with a Romanist on the way.

Monday, August 26

Just after breakfast arrived Mr. Newman, the gentleman engaged to keep the school for me. He had reached St. John's about 2 o'clock in the night, having left Cork on the 4th (Sunday) of August in the *Sandwich*. He has got a shocking bad hat and otherwise seems ill-provided about the head! Received a visit from a Mr. and Mrs. McCarty objecting to the proposed alteration in St. John's Church begun this morning — both eloquent and argumentative but rather too late.

Tried to move some of my books, but between a bad headache and misgivings and fears about the school little was done.

On unpacking my goods received by *Martha Harrison* found to my dismay that the crockery ware and glass was not sent, or at least has not arrived, but instead there is a box of books, a present from Mr. Leicester, a clergyman near Liverpool.

Dined at home with Messrs. Palairet and Newman and find that Mr. Newman requires new meats and drinks — our sumptuary laws dreadfully violated: beer and wine crept upon the frugal board, not to mention two dishes &c.

Tuesday, August 27

Went down before breakfast to see the alterations in progress in St. John's Church. Got to the Rectory before Mr. Bridge had descended from his chamber. Heard of the arrival of the [. . .] from England with Mr. Newman's books. Went over the late Chief Justice's residence with Mr. Scott, the agent of Mr. Brooking, to whom the house belongs, and made an offer for the purchase, viz. £1,000 currency minus £100 for repair.

Wrote a letter to the Rev. Mr. [Thomas] Boone at Twillingate, proposing to him that he should go to Port de Grave in place of Mr. Vicars, in case Mr. Vicars should go to Harbour Grace. Heard of complaints against the Rev. Mr. [William] Bowman of Fogo, charging him with intoxication. Received yesterday a visit from the Rev.

Mr. [James] Gilchrist of Greenspond, who has left his mission on account of ill health. All these things are against me.

Wednesday, August 28

After prayers said by Palairet, I started with faithful Bridge in a waggon for Torbay en route to Pouch Cove. Reached Torbay soon after twelve and found a boat and crew from Pouch Cove awaiting our arrival, 10 fine fellows willing and able. The harbour of Torbay is full 3 miles in length; the banks of either side are green and cultivated to a considerable extent, and the cultivation is evidently improving and spreading. The banks themselves are the usual hard, stern rocks, running into the sea in unbroken, irregular masses, leaving no beach except at the head of the bay. They are not lofty. On getting out of the bay, we found the shore more lofty, and the dark, irregular, unapproachable cliffs in some places are quite awful. You can hardly help thinking of the certain and speedy destruction of any vessel, however great and strong, which might be driven against them, of which, alas! there have [been] many sad proofs and instances. The stratification is most irregular — in some places quite horizontal, and again close adjoining quite perpendicular — in other places bent on curves or gradually passing from the perpendicular to the horizontal. So that these mighty masses, now so impenetrable and immovable, must at some time have been twisted and tossed about as within the strong man's hand or almost as the pliant and plastic waves of the restless sea. There are two or three places where red rocks peep out, noted by the sailors of course and named Redhead.

After a stiff pull with very little help from the wind, we reached Pouch Cove about 3 o'clock. This place has not been settled above 50 years and is what the people call a very wild place, being open to the sea, and in a strong northeast wind unapproachable. There was quite a fleet of fishing boats lying in the cove, unfortunately having no employment for want of bait. To prove the cold, dangerous nature of the coast, it was mentioned that in the autumn of last year there were lying 33 boats at their moorings in the evening, and the following morning only 3 remained that were worth saving. The people all build their own boats and get all materials (except nails) in their woods. The landing was rather difficult, there being no beach, and the swell dashing the boat at one moment with violence against the rude ladders leading to the stage, and then carrying it away back again to the distance of some feet. However, there were many kind and stout hands held out to assist me, with ropes &c, and I got safely on the first round of the ladder. A gun was fired in honour of my arrival, and in ascending the stage I found all the children of the schools, with the master at their head, drawn up under a flake to welcome me.

They preceded me to the church, which I found in a most filthy, dilapidated state from its having been used as the daily schoolroom. A schoolroom with dwelling for the master attached is now in progress, at a convenient distance from the church. The master, a Mr. Aldington from Cheltenham, is a young, unmarried man

(26) who has been settled there about 4 months and is very useful and much beloved by the people. He has instructed the children to make the responses very correctly and becomingly, to sing psalms and chant the Glorias. He is in a dangerous position, in consequence of his popularity, being also good looking and well dressed and well mannered &c. He lives in a very humble cottage rented for him by the Newfoundland School Society and receives as his stipend £60. A little boy resides in his house named [Mathew], son of a chymist and druggist and living in the High St., Oxford. He ran away from his parents and getting on board a trader came to Newfoundland, and in some way got shipped at Pouch Cove and is now supported by the schoolmaster, on whom he attends as companion and servant.

After visiting the church and announcing our purpose of holding a service at 5 o'clock, we went to the residence of our host, a patriarchal planter and fisherman named [John] Sullivan. He is the father of the settlement, being the first person who regularly established himself about 40 years ago, at which time the land was covered with trees. There now are the bare fields, dwellings and gardens. He has three sons married whom, with their families, he still maintains as when they were children, some living under his roof, others in cottages hard by. We had the usual dinner of scrods and tea with plenty of plum bread, well buttered. Mrs. Sullivan only partook with us, as Skipper had not returned from St. John's.

At 5 o'clock, we had our service, which was crowded. Three children were admitted into the Church who had before been baptized by Mr. Bridge. I addressed them on the text St. Matthew 28: 18, 19, 20.[7] After the service, we took tea and fish with another planter named [William] Williams, a Welshman, a few years ago a drunkard and retailer of ardent spirits, now a teetotaller. He is thriving and bringing up a family something like his neighbour Sullivan. The schoolmaster, Mr. Bridge and Mr. and Mrs. Williams were the party. This reputation of fish as a meal brings to my mind the fare of the apostles, tho' I expect in other matters, our tea and bread, we were far better provided than the holy apostles or their blessed Master.

After tea, we repaired again to Sullivan's, where after prayers I retired to rest in a little room which had been decked, for the occasion I presume, with counterpanes and curtains spread on the floor. There was a very clean, comfortable bed. I had [a] most refreshing sleep but was awakened early by the surging of the sea, which had become heavy by reason of the wind. I rose early and went to the schoolmaster's house, examined the school buildings in progress and prepared for the service in the church at 8 o'clock. This was well attended as last night. Three children were baptized. I addressed them on St. Mark and read the accounts of David's care for building the temple and encouraging them to attempt the renovation of their church. I

[7]St. Matthew 28: 18-20: And Jesus came and spake unto them, saying, All power is given unto me in heaven and in earth, Go ye therefore, and teach all nations, baptizing them in the name of the Father, and of the Son, and of the Holy Ghost: Teaching them to observe all things whatsoever I have commanded you: and, lo, I am with you alway, even unto the end of the world.

also warned them against the Romanists. The Holy Communion was administered, but only 8 persons received.

After this service, we administered the Holy Sacrament to a sick woman in a private house. Then we breakfasted at the schoolmaster's house (I and Mr. Bridge). The morning was very wet, but we determined to start and accordingly, soon after 12 o'clock, we descended to the romantic stage, accompanied by many women and children, who took a very affectionate farewell. As many as 20 guns were fired in honour of the event. The Skipper (Sullivan) himself took the helm (having come home late the evening before) and, having a fine crew, many of them the same persons who brought us, we again launched out, taking the schoolmaster with us. Six of the crew were unmarried men, and they would not let the married men work. The only refreshment they had or desired (and the day was very hot and the work hard, for there was a great swell) was a small barrel of water, about 12 gallons, and a little biscuit. It was amusing to see them lift this barrel to their mouths and drink out of a bunghole as cheerfully and contentedly as if the contents had been nectar or *eau de vie*.[8] Certainly, the effects of the temperance societies in this aspect are wonderful and blessed indeed. Ardent spirits seem almost vanished, and other fermented liquors are little known or desired. Water when at work and tea at home seem to supply all their needs and gratify all their wishes. And these are stout men, exposed to all weathers at all hours, enduring great labours and fatigue. To this temperance they appear to have added brotherly kindness certainly and, I hope, to brotherly kindness charity. They expressed and displayed great regard for their schoolmaster and said if he stayed away long they must man a boat to bring him home. They are kind and brotherly to each other and hospitable to strangers.

The wind and sea were against us; we did not reach Torbay till 6 o'clock. There was the same difficulty in ascending the steps of the flake. I went first with success, but the schoolmaster missed the step and fell into the sea. He was quickly caught by 2 stout men by the collar of his cloak and held up with his legs dangling in the water. The only danger then was that the boat, in returning, might crush him against the ladder, but the men were very careful and vigilant, and I being just above him seized his collar and helped to drag him up in time to escape the blow. There was no harm beyond the wetting of his lower extremities and of his hat, which fell into the sea, and the tearing of his cloak.

We found faithful Clancy, Mr. Bridge's servant, waiting for us with the horse waggon and reached St. John's about 6 o'clock, having left Torbay at 4 o'clock. Found a note from Mr. Vicars, asking me to baptize his child on Sunday next, and from Mr. Scott, declining my offer of £900 currency for the house, and from Mrs. Cowan, asking me to buy her late husband's books.

[8] *Eau de vie*: a fruit brandy produced by fermentation and double distillation.

Friday, August 30

Went down to Mr. Bridge's to see the progress of the alterations in St. John's Church, which appeared satisfactory. Said the prayers at St. Thomas's Church. Received many calls of enquiry about the school. Wrote to Mr. Vicars and Mr. Scott — called on Mr. Spearman, Mr. Simms.

Saturday, August 31

After much deliberation and consulting with Mr. Blackman about the wind and weather determined not to go to Port de Grave. Assisted two of the students in sorting and arranging some of the tracts. Dined at home with Palairet and Newman.

Appendix A

Letters to the Rev. William Scott on Church Architecture
Halifax, Nova Scotia, 1 July 1844

My Dear Scott,[1]

The smoke is rising from the steamer which is to convey us this evening to Newfoundland. I see it from my window, and very black smoke it is, I assure you.

I shall very much want plans and of churches, for I find the Cathedral in St. John's is not yet begun and I do not think there is any prospect of commencing it this year: and indeed I am not anxious at all to hasten it. You would do me a very great kindness if you would procure for me all useful modern ecclesiastical books of architecture, not very expensive (except the books published by the Architectural Society in Oxford),[2] and especially any good designs of wooden churches. A Mr. Penmore of Rugby promised to give me drawings and descriptions of wooden churches in Norway, but I did not receive them.

I would also be much obliged if you would send me a portable font with the plate.

These things should, if you please, be sent direct to Newfoundland.

I have said so much about the miserable imitation fonts in this place and neighbourhood that I feel constrained to make one of the churches here a present of a good one, and as nobody knows anything of such matters here it seems necessary that two or 3 full-sized or half-sized models in wood should be sent over. They must be plain but large. I am afraid to have a font actually made in England lest any accident should happen to break or injure it. Do you think you could kindly undertake to

[1]Rev. William Scott (1813-1872), a fellow student of Feild's at Queen's College Oxford, where he took an MA in 1839, was also a Tractarian. He was later vicar of St. Olave's, Jewry, London, with St. Martin Pomeroy, London, in 1860. He edited the *Christian Remembrancer*, 1841-68, and was one of the founders of the *Saturday Review*.

[2]The Society was founded in 1839 as the Society for Promoting the Study of Gothic Architecture. It was renamed the Oxford Architectural Society in 1848 and refounded as the Oxford Architectural and Historical Society in 1860.

have two or three models made and directed to the Archdeacon Willis, Halifax, Nova Scotia?

Mr. Cecil Way of Liverpool would, I am sure, kindly help in forwarding anything to me or for me. Another vacancy has occurred in Newfoundland since I left England: at Harbour Grace, the next place in importance to St. John's. Can you find or recommend a clergyman?

Audland promised to send me the publications of the Oxford Architectural Society, but they did not reach me. A new church is just about to be built in Bermuda.

St. John's, Newfoundland, 11 July 1844

I trust that the commission with which I ventured to trouble you, relating to fonts, will not be attended with much difficulty or trouble — or if such should be the case, I beg you will set it aside altogether.

I am very anxious to obtain more good models or drawings, or both, for I find there is the same deficiency and ignorance here as in Nova Scotia. In the principal church of St. John's (tell it not in Gath[3] or elsewhere) it is still the custom, when a baptism occurs in the church, to bring in a basin with water and put it on the altar ! The font required for the church in Halifax must not have a large base and should not be very high, on account of the confined place in which it must be placed; at present the imitation font stands behind the pulpit, which of course is immediately before the altar. Van Voorst's drawings would be acceptable.[4]

I would be glad also if you could procure for me two or three alms basins, one silver and one pewter flagon, without a spout or lip, in other respects similar to yours. There is neither flagon nor alms basin in the church at St. John's, at which I administered the sacrament last Sunday. Please to inform me in what way the alms are collected in your church, boxes or bags? Here they have broken copper and wooden boxes fixed at the ends of long sticks, which are all brought to the altar and deposited in a most unseemly manner (as disturbing the arrangements etc.) one after the other by the priest. It is consequently very difficult to bring them reverently or present them humbly. If you should be able to comply with my wishes respecting the fonts, please to direct them to Mr. Cunard instead of to Archdeacon Willis, as suggested in my first application.

With respect to our Cathedral, the prospects are dark and disheartening. While the Roman Catholics are proceeding rapidly with an immense edifice in a most commanding situation (the cost of which cannot be less, I should think in this country, than 50,000), we have not been able to make a commencement; only cut stone has been ordered and brought from Ireland for the accompanying frightful structure

[3]2 Samuel, 1: 20: Tell it not in Gath, publish it not in the streets of Askelon; lest the daughters of the Philistines rejoice, lest the daughters of the uncircumcised triumph.

[4]See F.A. Paley, *Illustrations of Baptismal Fonts*. London: John Van Voorst, 1844.

— the opposite side is precisely similar. What is to be done? Could you send me a ground plan of the new church in Westminster (Broadway, I think)?

22 August 1844

Your kind and acceptable letter of the 2nd of August reached me yesterday (with 16 others) by the steam packet. Before I received these numerous letters (expecting a rather large arrival), I had taken time, as they say, by the forelock,[5] and had bestowed a great deal of my tediousness upon you in a very long letter which I have sent together with drawings of our projected cathedral and drawings of the wooden churches shewing the manner in which they are commonly constructed and asking, of course, a great deal of counsel and advice.

This letter will contain a report of proceedings of the Building Committee, which I have required them to draw up, with a debtor and creditor account and a plan of the churchyard with the addition made to it for the site of the Cathedral. By this account it appears that the money already paid amounts to £3,764 14 3 and that £500 more will very soon be required to pay for the last instalment of cut stone, nearly the whole of which has been delivered, so that at least the sum of £4,300 currency, about £3,686 sterling, will have been expanded, or you may say has been expended, merely to purchase the ashlar and ornamental stone. And there it lies on the spot — it must be used and there is nobody here that can alter the cuttings or facings. It would be quite impossible to dispose of it. Who would buy it — who would have it for nothing? Moreover, the land given by the Governor, exchanged away for the present site, was valued at £1.150 cur. — about £986 (say £1,000) sterling. This statement, I hope, by help of the accompanying paper, will be clear to you — and it will be clear that nearly, if not quite £5,000 sterling, will have been expended in procuring the site and outside and ornamental stone, and I do not know that more money has been spent than necessary, or that the same quantity of any proper stone could have been procured for a less sum. But observe there is no stone to spare, so that we cannot enlarge our plan, using the present or any similar drawings, without sending to Ireland for more stone, and you see the enormous expense attending it.

What does it avail to congratulate one that the Cathedral is not begun, as if I could alter the plan or make a choir and expect the rest to follow by degrees: *movit Amphion lapides canendo*?[6] I have no materials, no means for building a choir, and cannot get them. The only thing that appears to be possible is to build the body of the church as represented in the drawing, lessening the windows a little (though any alterations of the windows would require fresh stones), omitting the tower alto-

[5]To take time by the forelock: to seize an opportunity. The Latin fabulist Phaedrus described opportunity or occasion as being bald, except for a long forelock, a personification illustrated in Renaissance emblem books and applied to Time.

[6]Horace, *Odes*, 3.11: *movit Amphion lapides canendo* — Amphion moved the rocks by singing.

gether and adding a wooden chancel. We might possibly make a stone choir with our present materials — but I do not think the committee and subscribers would consent, and we have no stone for an arch between chancel and nave. Indeed, I am sure they would not, and there would be no means at all for constructing the wooden nave which, of the size required, would cost nearly £3,000, as Mr. [Archdeacon Edward] Wix must know from the cost of his neat little church [St. Thomas's] in this neighbourhood. It would cost at least £5,000 to finish and fit up such a building as at present designed, and (besides what I may furnish) they have not much above £1,000 promised.

Here is a pretty colonial mess, out of which at present I cannot see how to escape. It is an occasion merely for desiring counsel and asking direction and exercising patience. I do not know that I can add anything more in way of explanation. Together with these papers relating to the Cathedral, I send also the developments I spoke of — of pulpit reading desk etc. drawn by Mr. Bridge. Perhaps Mr. Wix will recognize and acknowledge one of them. Will you thank Mrs. Wix for her kind and encouraging note. The *Hawk*,[7] if here, might, I dare say, have been let to the judges this autumn — but they have already, I believe, engaged their vessel.

You will find in my other letter an answer to all your kind enquiries about plaster, fonts, etc. The font for Halifax [is] to be sent to Halifax direct and that for me to St. John's direct and therefore, of course, by different ships. Let me hear that you have received both my letters and taken my matters into your grave consideration. I place great reliance about your kindness, fully proved, and your skill not doubted. Plaster certainly will not stand, and there is no lime in the country. The stone about St. John's is the most impracticable you can conceive (*infames scopulos*[8] Palairet calls them). Do not trouble yourself more about the Norway churches — though I dare say the admonition comes too late. I quite assent to all your arguments about the fonts, especially the seventh. I know [Barder] better than Formby does; his ideas and views are all from poetry and music and would hardly suit the fogs and frost of N.F.L. But let him try — I expect our schoolmaster Mr. Newman in a few days. He is coming in the same ship with Dr. [Michael Anthony] Fleming. I can only repeat my thanks with blessings for all your kind and generous exertions.

August 1844

I owe you great thanks for both what you have written to me and what you have written for or about me. I hardly know which to be most grateful for and most to admire, your letter in the *English Churchman* or that in your own manuscript, which you have sent to gladden my eyes and comfort my heart by this mail. I need hardly

[7]The *Hawk*, a square-topsail schooner of about 70 tons, was fitted up as a church as well as a ship and could accommodate a congregation in the coves and harbours where there were no churches.

[8]Horace, *Odes*, 1.3: *Infames scopulos* — Unspeakable crags.

say I hope your letter in the *Churchman* was widely circulated, for it must, I think, open the minds and hearts of any who read it while I feast in private upon the contents of your communications, so full and interesting, to myself.

I have so much to say to you that I must proceed to business without further preface. (1) As to the ship — I thank you most heartily for the interest and pains you have taken in seeing her duly equipped. Hawkins speaks in terms of great admiration of your exertions. You seem to have thought of everything which is essential and necessary. I wish some person could have contributed a small organ and you could have sent your friend Jackson to recover his health and direct our services here. This climate is universally praised as very healthy, and at this season of the year there is little difference between Newfoundland and England to the outward bodily feelings, except that on the whole we are a little colder here, and the changes of the weather are more frequent and rapid than even in the old country.

While on this subject I may just mention that the land is far more cultivable and (in the neighbourhood of St. John's) far more cultivated than I expected to find it. Wheat is not grown, but there are splendid crops of grass just now being cut. We have as yet no seeds, no ripe gooseberries, raspberries or currents; strawberries and potatoes just coming in, lilacs and laburnums just going out. This for the curious in vegetables and all others whom it may concern; all I wish to be known is that the place and climate are decidedly healthful and that persons unable to bear the confinement of towns may expect here to be braced and strengthened as much as in any county village of England.

The only thing that grieves me about the church ship is the expense, which I gather from Hawkins's acct. will be nearly £800, and I dare be certain there is nothing superfluous. I hope somebody has thought about having her ensured. It will not be possible, I am informed, to change her name, not even to convert *Hawk* into *Hawkins*. Eden, of course, is the name of names if it can be so contrived,[9] but next to that Ernest Hawkins would be very pleasant and appropriate; but I believe the name of a ship is generally considered as unchangeable by addition or otherwise, as our baptismal names — under whatever name she will be mush prized and honoured and, I trust, will not be or be deemed a ravening bird of prey but the herald of peace and consolation and of a good hope through grace. We shall anxiously look for her arrival about the end of this month.

I have not heard from Carden since I left England but infer from your silence he has received the plate I intended for his use. He will, I believe, pay the bill out of monies he holds for me, but if there is any delay, I beg you will kindly inform me, and I will send the amount due by bill or otherwise as you may direct.

I gladly accept your proposal to get the font for Halifax made in England. The chief difficulties I had about such an arrangement lay in the risk and expense of

[9]Feild refers to his friend Rev. Robert Eden (1804-1886), Rector of Leigh in the Diocese of London, who had previously given the schooner *Emma Eden*, which was unsuitable for Newfoundland. He was later Primus of Scotland.

transmitting it. I wish it, if you please, to be plain, not lofty, and not requiring a large base; plain because I cannot afford an ornamental one and because an ornamental one would be less suitable, and not lofty because it must stand in the centre of an aisle which is confined, and not one inch of pew room can be spared. I will thank you also to have one made for me to be sent direct to St. John's. Except the marble font erected by Archdeacon Wix, there is not one in Newfoundland. There is, however, this excuse that there is no stone yet found on the island capable of being cut for such a purpose, and the Roman Catholics are in the same predicament as ourselves. I have ordered one to be made for St. John's church of limestone which has been imported from Ireland for the Cathedral, but I very much fear there is no mason who can cut it decently.

Now with respect to the ill-starred Cathedral (if I may so speak without irreverence). I have already said in one of my letters home that the stone for the whole outside and for all the windows, doors, pinnacles, buttresses, etc., has been imported ready cut and prepared from Ireland, so that the exterior seems as much determined, supposing we have money to complete it, as though it were already built. But the fact is there are no means to complete or proceed with it, on this or any other plan, and I can see no disposition on the part of the people to come forward with additional subscriptions at all adequate to the object.

I should like very well to begin with a choir, but in the meantime there is a want of accommodation for the congregation, and the old wooden church is fast falling to pieces. I intend in a short time to send a report of the state of our funds with our proceedings, prospects and plans to England to ascertain how far the plan can be modified or altered so as to allow [still] of the stone now imported being used and obtain something more of an ecclesiastical character without additional expense and without loss of room inside. No pillars are contemplated but a flat roof of 100 ft. by 50 ft., no chancel or choir, no font, no tracery in any windows.

Have you ever seen drawings of the Cathedral Ch. of St. Magnus in Kirkwall? I believe there was a wood engraving of it in the *Ch. of England Magazine*, I think of April this year. I was much struck with its solidity and simplicity. I thought it admirably suited to this climate and country — but then it has large arches and tiers, etc., inside with a clerestory. I wish you would look at it if you have an opportunity. I should like also to know the dimensions and arrangements of your own church and of that at Broadway, Westminster. With respect to tracery, it must be observed there is no stone in the country which will cut for such purposes, no persons who can cut it — and, if cut, the weather would quickly "perish" it unless it were granite or the hardest limestone.

Nothing of the kind has been attempted or designed by the Roman Catholics here in their cathedral. Theirs will be an immense building of a cruciform shape, with an ambulatory all about it, the windows of the ambulatory square-headed and of the Cathedral itself round, but without tracery or ornamental work of any kind. The ambulatory is a lean-to. There will be two towers at the west end. When completed, it will be fitted up with pews and galleries. The thickness of the inner walls which support the roof is 4 feet and the walls of [the] ambulatory 3/9. The ambulatory will, I presume, be used for processions but is chiefly intended to protect the interior building and its inmates from the weather. Dr. Fleming, their bishop, is not here but is expected shortly and no doubt will come well supplied with money. Indeed, he seems to command any sums for any purposes he pleases. His own estates near St. John's are said to have cost many thousand pounds. One was purchased for him this week. Their cathedral will cost full £50,000 when completed and fitted up.

You should understand that building here, in stone, is 50 per cent dearer than in England. Stone and lime are both imported from Ireland. There is, of course, abundance of stone in Newfoundland, in fact the whole island is stone, but they either have not found [any] in the neighbourhood of St. John's or they do not know how to work any quarries of good building stone. Rough walls are sometimes built of this country stone, but these generally fall in 3 or 4 years unless built very thick and carefully looked after. Their mason's work cannot be continued more than 6 or 5 months in the year, and if walls are left unfinished, they will be probably much injured in the winter. The two towers of the Roman Catholic Cathedral were from this cause obliged to be taken down several feet this year at a loss, it is said, of from £700 to £800. The wages of workmen are nearly double those in England. There are no builders, properly so called, in the country, persons in turn keeping a number of hands employed and a stock of materials. You could not find a wagon-load of stone in St. John's. You will now form some idea of the difficulties in which we are placed in respect of our cathedral.

Now with respect to our wooden churches, you will easily gather from what has been already said that outside plaster would not stand the weather at all. Lime also is very dear, being all imported, as I said, from Ireland. Plaster can be and is used inside, as in England, and there are cornices and other ornaments in the houses similar to those home, but more expensive.

The common way of constructing the churches is this. The frame is cut in the woods and hauled out in the winter over the snow by the inhabitants of the settlement who require it. You understand that all our timber is either fir or spruce. When the pieces of framing are brought to the spot, they are put together and put up by the natives. They vary from 4 to 8 inches in thickness, the sills commonly a little thicker than the uprights. The frames sometimes stand on a footing of stone, i.e., a wall of rough stones laid on the ground, with or without mortar, and sometimes are only supported on a few short, stout poles just sufficiently near for that purpose to keep the frame from touching the ground. The latter is the cheaper plan and therefore more commonly adopted. The frame thus put up is covered with rough planks, also cut from the woods (or sometimes of American spruce or pine), and these again with clapboards or weather boards with a feathered edge and lapping one over the other and presenting a succession of horizontal lines which at first is very strange and disagreeable to English eyes. The frames are covered also inside with plain boards of planks called cieling [*sic*] but sometimes are plastered. These are generally American [New Brunswick] . Hard woods are unknown in this part of the country, and the American fir is very inferior to the Memel commonly used in England.

The roofs are covered with shingle (of wood), which is of course very light, and being painted looked like stone tile and is not any way objectionable. The outside walls require to be painted to preserve them. Nothing like an ornamental timber roof has yet been attempted, partly because there is little large or good wood on the island and partly because no persons know how to make them, and but few desire them. The desire is to have flat cielings across the building, either of plank or designed in plaster. These are generally tie beams at the first side-piece about halfway down, which are merely nailed to the couples rafters and are only rough sticks or poles, but there are no ties at the wall plates. Light open roofs might easily be constructed if we had any good models or drawings — not difficult or expensive. Such drawings I very much want.

Galleries are common — almost universal — and one excuse is made for them which will not apply in England. The frames, as I have said, are merely placed on a footing of stone or on poles and are not otherwise united or fastened to the ground. They are consequently liable to be shaken or moved by the winds, which are frequent and powerful in this country, and require to be strengthened. Now the upright posts of the galleries run up from the floor to the roof at intervals of perhaps 10 or 12 feet, and cross pieces to support the front of the galleries go from one post to the other — all the way from the east to the west end and contribute much to the support of the frame.

The floors are always of board, and generally double, as the wind circulates freely under the floor. The upper floors, seats and ends of seats are generally of American spruce or pine. A stove is considered indispensable. The windows are (strange to say) large and numerous without mullions or muntins and filled with large square panes. Diamond frames are unknown. All our glass is imported from England. The heads of the windows are either pointed or round. The walls when completed are from 6 to 10 inches thick. Sometimes the clapboards are put on the frames without underboards, of course for economy. You might erect a decent shell of a church 50 ft. by 30 with the help of the inhabitants for £150 (without a tower).

The fitting up is generally execrable, for besides the galleries which run to the very east end (there being no chancel) we have narrow, high pews running up also to the east end and anchoring the rails of the altar, the pulpit, reading desk and clerk's seat standing in the middle aisle, not small by degrees and beautifully less — but rising from a high clerk's desk to the preacher's towering eminence (a bad eminence as Palairet calls it). All these, of course, are immediately in front of the altar and last window. Sometimes they are within the altar rails and against the east wall, the communion table being in front of the reading desk.

I send you herewith drawings explanatory of our wooden temples and also of the extraordinary developments of pulpit, reading desk etc. which have been produced under the auspices of different missionaries — and I think you may make them the subject of a communication to the Camden Society[10] or to the Oxford Architectural Society. I shall probably myself send to Parker a similar detail if I can find time. There are now, I suppose, 20 churches at least on the island which are at a stand for want of funds to complete them and several others requiring repairs and alterations which the poor people cannot accomplish, and if I had means at my command I might see them furnished or altered in a decent manner.

I may speak now on the subject of a residence. The Governor (Sir John Harvey) has very kindly offered to present me, his bishop, with an acre of ground near to the gate of Government House and to St. Thomas's Church, exceedingly eligible for such a purpose. On one side is a public road and on another a large open space leading only to Government House, on the remaining two sides land belonging to the government, never likely to be built on. I must send a plan of the ground to England that I may get advice as to the commencement of a modest collegiate building. I could build on one or all four sides of a parallelogram. The chief, indeed the only objection is that it is at a distance from the projected cathedral. It is only to step across a road, and that not a public one for carriages, and I should be in the churchyard of St. Thomas's Church. If I could change the site of the cathedral and make St. Thomas's the seat of the Bishop the situation would be perfect. Give me opinions as to the propriety to such a change.

I was, of course, very sorry to lose [Thurder], though I never considered him fixed or to be fixed. His musical talents would have been highly valuable. Church music is not cultivated or understood here, but I doubt not would have admirable effect if well introduced. How often have I remembered with pleasure the services in your church and sighed to think I shall perhaps never equal them in my cathedral. I have begun a daily service in the church near here and am happy to say the Governor always attends in the morning, and I require the students at the Theological Institution to attend.

I have just returned from visiting some of the distant churches in the Diocese and have been extremely interested with the country and people. I was absent 7 days and in that time preached 9 times and administered the sacrament 3 times. At two country places (fishing settlements) all the communicants, men and women (45 in one case and 21 in the other), came up to the rails in succession to shake hands with me. Not a word was spoken, but tears stood in many eyes, and the shake of the hand was right hearty and affectionate, and I could almost fancy we had complied with the apostolic ordinance "Salute ye one another ἐν ἁγίῳ φιλήματι [*en hagioi philemati*]".[11]

[10]Camden Society: named after the early English historian William Camden, it was founded in 1838 to publish early historical and literary materials, both unpublished manuscripts and new editions of printed books.

[11]2 Corinthians, 13:12: Greet one another with an holy kiss.

At these settlements, though there is a church and considerable population of Ch. people, the clergyman's visits are of necessity few and far between. Palairet, who resides at St. John's with me, has the care of 5 outports, one of them 18 miles and the nearest eight miles off. Last Sunday he walked ten miles out and 10 miles back to perform one service at a place called Petty Harbour. Neither of his other churches [had] a clergyman on that day. An old man who came from a distant settlement (an island) to attend a funeral where Palairet officiated begged him to ask the Bishop to send a clergyman to their island (where there is already a church which, I think, has not been visited by a clergyman since the late Bishop consecrated the churchyard there and added that he and his [mission] would creep on their hands and knees to such a gentleman as him (Palairet). At every place which I visited there was the same cry, the same prayer, send us a clergyman. In almost all the settlements too the churches are unfinished, and if there were means at my command I might prevent, in many cases, the abominations of galleries and pews which are now likely to overspread the diocese and that any most offensive shape being permanently sold or let out by yearly rent. How am I to prevent this where there are no means of either furnishing the churches or maintaining them in repair, much less of paying a clergyman?

I must now bring this lengthy and, I fear, somewhat incoherent detail to a close. I could send you drawings of our churches, but I dare say Mrs. Wix has drawings of St. Thomas's and [will] carefully explain to you the mode of its construction. What do you think of having a wooden church as a model or parts of one (windows, roof and bench ends) made in England? I am inclined to think single light windows of the Norman or Early English would be best. Will you kindly shew this to Hawkins and any persons who may be interested. I beg to send my kind regards and blessing to Mrs. Scott, so I bless you, my dear friend.

Your obliged and affectionate,
Edward Newfoundland

Appendix B

Report of the Cathedral Building Committee

The Committee appointed to superintend the erection of the projected cathedral and parish church in St. John's think it due to the subscribers to make a report f the progress and prospects of the work entrusted to them at this time.

The attention of the committee was, in the first place, directed to procuring the most eligible site, not merely for the present population but also, and especially, for the generations to come. For it must always be remembered that the Cathedral is designed and intended not to meet present wants and desires only but to embrace a provision for those which the lapse of years and an increasing community will create. It is well known that this object was surrounded with many and great difficulties; but with the blessing of God, they have all been surmounted, and a site has been obtained immediately north of the churchyard — the eligibility and convenience of which are universally perceived and admitted. It has been obtained in exchange for certain portions of Crown Land which were granted to the Lord Bishop of Newfoundland and his successors, through the kindness of His Excellency Sir John Harvey, to whom the committee are glad of an opportunity to reiterate, in their own name and that of their brethren throughout the colony, the expression of their warmest thanks. The site thus obtained has been secured as the property of the Church forever, by regular and legal conveyance to the Bishop of the Diocese, in whom, and his successors, it is vested in trust for the uses and purposes above-named.

Drawings and elevations, prepared by Mr. Purcell, were approved by the late Bishop [Aubrey Spencer] and adopted by the committee for a stone edifice to be built in such a manner as shall be suited to this climate and best ensure its durability and permanence.

The committee have contracted for a sufficient quantity of Cork limestone of the best quality to complete the external facings of the walls, with the tower, spire, buttresses &c., according to the plans and drawings submitted to them, to the thickness of nine inches all over the building, with a sufficient bond in at least every 10 feet. The walls are to be two feet, six inches thick and to be completed with the stone of this country. All the mouldings, arches and ornamental stonework are included in this contract. The whole of the above stone was contracted for at two shillings sterling per superficial foot, delivered, shipped and stowed at Cork; and the amount to be paid to the contractor, Mr. Purcell, on this account was two thousand, six hundred pounds sterling. An agent (Thomas S. Reeves, Esq.) was appointed at Cork to measure the stone as delivered by the contractor. The contractor is bound to repair, at his own expense, any fractures or damage that may happen to the stone before it is delivered to the committee in St. John's.

Nearly the whole of the cut stone contracted for from Ireland has been now supplied and safely deposited in the cathedral-yard. Mr. Purcell has received £2,100 sterling, and the balance of his contract, amounting to £500 sterling, will be paid to him within three months after the committee shall have been certified by their agent in Cork that the last cargo of stone he is bound to supply has been delivered and shipped at that port. £1006 16 10 have been paid for freights, duty &c., the particulars of which will appear in the annexed account.

Of the sum of £3,964 15s. currency subscribed for in St. John's (payable in five annual instalments, of which the last is due on the 1st of June 1846), £1,817 6 11 have been received by the treasurer and expended on account of stone, &c, together with £500 stg. granted by the Society for the Propagation of the Gospel in Foreign Parts, and £799 19 8 sterling collected in England by the Rev. Mr. Bridge. £331 15 4 cy. have been advanced by the committee and treasurer to meet payments for the stone and the expenses incidental to its importation. A list of subscribers will be immediately published, shewing both the amounts promised and the sums actually paid up the date in Newfoundland. The committee beg to invite the particular attention of members of the Church in Newfoundland to the liberality of friends in England and to tender to those friends their cordial and most grateful acknowledgements. The sum of £500 sterling given by the Society for Promoting Christian Knowledge was reserved by the Lord Bishop of Jamaica (our then Diocesan) to be paid, with interest, "only for the actual completion of the church," and the amount of that grant, with the interest thereon up to this time, is now in the hands of the Bishop of Newfoundland.

The committee have great pleasure in announcing that the Lord Bishop of the Diocese has engaged to contribute £1,000 sterling from the subscriptions of his friends in England and £250 on his own account to meet the same amounts subscribed and paid in Newfoundland, or instalments of those sums to meet equal instalments here. Several gentlemen of St. John's have offered to increase or continue their subscriptions beyond the amounts standing against their names. The third annual instalment of local contributions, due since the 1st of June last, will be more than absorbed by the liquidation of the advances already referred to and the cash payments to Mr. Purcell on account of stone. The instalments subscribed for, for the years 1845 and 1846, will realize about £1,200 or £1,300 currency.

It has been thought expedient to send the plans and drawings to England to obtain the advice and the approval of skilful and kind friends and contributors there. In the meantime, it is desired and intended, if means be provided, to procure rubble stone and other materials without delay and to level and prepare the ground during the ensuing fall, in hopes that the building may be commenced in the spring of next year. This, however, must depend on the punctuality with which the promised instalments are paid and the liberality of new subscribers, and therefore the committee earnestly solicit contributions (besides money) of stone, sand and other materials from the members of the Church, entreating them to remember whose work it is they are anxious to further and whose interests they desire to promote — the work of God and the interests of His people.

St. John's Vestry Room
October 1844

Appendix C

A Charge Delivered to the Clergy of the Diocese of Newfoundland

Dear and Reverend Brethren:

At your request and for your use, I commit to print so much of my late charge as relates to the public services of the Church. The general exhortations to uniformity with which my charge was prefaced are omitted, not as being unimportant in themselves but as, happily, unnecessary in your case. The same remark applies to some sentences of admonition and encouragement at the close. However I might have deemed it proper or necessary "to stir up your pure minds by way of remembrance [2 Peter, 3: 1]," the intercourse I have since enjoyed with you has convinced me that you fully appreciated, if not anticipated on these points, all my wishes and views. To repeat, then, such general remarks and exhortations would needlessly swell a publication more large and lengthy in its present state than desirable and cause me additional labour and expense, neither of which I can well afford. I trust I may with propriety, as I can in all sincerity, take leave of you, in the Apostle's words, "joying and beholding your order and the stedfastness of your faith in Christ [Colossians 2: 5]."

I remain,

Reverend and Dear Brethren,
Your affectionate brother and servant,
Edward Newfoundland
St. John's, October 4, 1844

* * *

I proceed now to tender you some information and advice on the public services in our Prayer Book and the manner of conducting and performing them, in doing which I shall be almost necessarily led to the kindred subject of church-arrangement.

First in order and first in importance are the public services of the Lord's Day. There are four distinct, though no longer necessarily separate, services for each Lord's Day, appointed and set forth in our Book of Common Prayer — 1st., the Order for Morning Prayer; 2d., the Litany; 3d., the Communion Office; and, 4th., the Order for Evening Prayer. The three offices of Morning Prayer, the Litany and Holy Communion are now commonly used, one in immediate succession after the other; but that they are really and essentially distinct services will appear from the following considerations.

1st., the Order for Morning Prayer is appointed to be and is frequently used on other days of the week as a complete service in itself, without either the Litany or Holy Communion. 2d., the Litany is, in many cathedral churches, still said at a considerable interval after the Order for Morning Prayer and may be used occasionally as a separate service under the direction of the Ordinary. It was to mark and maintain this distinction between the Order for Morning Prayer and the Litany that the rubric has been preserved after the third collect, "In Quires and Places where they sing, here followeth the Anthem." It is true that the rubric applies and should be observed when the Litany is not said, and both in the Morning and Evening Prayers; yet such, I am persuaded, was originally its object and use. And a very little reflection shews the purport and propriety of this direction; for if impatience of multiplied services and of frequent attendance at church on the part of the people or the paucity of ministers (which obliges their resorting to different parishes or places of worship) will not allow of the sufficient and intended interval, there is the more reason we should mark the distinction and difference of these services, I mean of the Order for Morning Prayer and the Litany, by some pause or change. It must, I think, have occurred to many, and would, no doubt, to more, if long custom had not made the practice familiar that to proceed at once from the Third Collect to the Litany without break or pause is somewhat abrupt and ungraceful and has, no doubt, given occasion (contrary, you see, to the mind and purpose of the Church) to the complaint sometimes made of the longsomeness [*sic*] of the Morning Prayers.

The fact is that the Litany is not part of the Order for Morning Prayer but a distinct service; and to mark, I say, the distinction (of course for the higher purpose of assisting our devotion) the anthem was directed here to be sung. By the help of this pause and refreshment, it is supposed we shall be better prepared for that solemn and affecting service of general supplication. Now, with this rubric, the meaning and propriety of which are so easily understood and readily approved (though I do not know that all are concerned to approve them), it cannot but seem strange — I will not say that no anthem or hymn should here be sung — but that, instead of it, a hymn should be inserted and used where there is no authority for one, and by no means the same necessity or propriety: for instance (as I have sometimes heard), after the Second Lesson and immediately before a canticle appointed by the Church or, more commonly, before the sermon, for which there is only the self-imposed necessity that the minister should then change his surplice for the black gown as if, when he ascended his pulpit to read his sermon or homily, he were no longer ministering in the Church. It is my wish that the distinction between the Order of Morning Prayer and the Litany should be noted and observed in places where they sing by an anthem or hymn after the Third Collect, as the rubric directs.

There is another method of marking the division of these services, once common if not universal, and still retained in a few churches — viz., by saying the Litany at a different desk, facing east and nearer to the east end of the church. This is called the litany desk and is still used in many cathedrals, particularly during the season of Lent. As, however, this custom has generally been discontinued and there is no direction on the point in the rubrics or canons, it would not, I think, be well to revive it (as changes are always attended with some inconvenience), though its propriety is evident when we consider the Litany as a distinct and separate service.

The practice, also, of facing to the east in saying the prayers has many recommendations, supposing the people generally can hear and follow the minister, which, with the help of their books, may easily be done. For in whatever character and capacity the priest or minister then acts, whether he be regarded as praying with or for the people or offering up his supplications together with theirs to the Throne of Grace as a deputation with or for them — in whatever light you regard his action, it is, surely, unnatural and unbecoming that he should, as it were, address himself to the congregation and people as instructing or encouraging or exhorting them.

I have noticed, however, one objection to this change of posture which, no doubt, where it applies, is of great weight; for we never should be satisfied if our people cannot hear and follow the prayers and say Amen at our giving of thanks. We do not and should not think it enough that God should hear and understand the minister's words or that the people should have a general knowledge only of the substance and subject of our petitions; for we believe it to be intended and ordered that they should pray with the spirit and with the understanding also; but — that grand and important point being secured — it may assist devotion and prevent that confusion which so often, I fear, exists in men's minds between instructions to and petitions for and with them — between preaching and praying — if they are taught not to direct their attention too closely and particularly to the minister. If, indeed, the people are, as they are directed, all devoutly kneeling, they will have no temptation to turn their eyes to him; and then at least it will be of no moment that his face is turned away from them.

It is sometimes, I know, urged that the clergyman must look around him to detect and prevent irregularities of behaviour; but this is, surely, a painful duty to be imposed upon him and which can hardly issue in the benefit of his flock, to say nothing of his own comfort and edification, a matter of some moment even to his congregation. The same reason, however, which I gave for not recommending a separate Litany desk induces me to request you not suddenly or abruptly to reverse your usual position in saying the Litany or other prayers; but to avoid that unmeaning and, to the clergyman at least, inconvenient arrangement of looking towards the whole congregation and being gazed at by them, I would recommend such an expedient as we have adopted in this church, to which, I conceive, no just objection can attach.[12]

The distinction between praying with or for our people and reading or preaching to them is or should be obvious; and with respect to preaching, it is sufficiently shewn by the pulpit facing, as it should do, to the people. The stand for the Holy Bible, from which the lessons are read, is not necessarily separated from the praying desk, though commonly in cathedrals and antient churches it was so; and there is a rubric which implies that a different minister and different position are required in reading as in preaching — different, I mean, from the prayers and psalms. "He that readeth," it is said, "so standing and turning himself as he may best be heard of all such as be present"[13] — and there is something surely pleasing and appropriate in the open bible laid in the centre of every church, a plain and perpetual testimony of the grounds of our faith and hope. Where this arrangement is not convenient on account of the want of space or the difficulty of a single minister leaving and returning to the desk, or from any other cause, I would recommend that (the praying-desk being placed as in this church) another desk be joined to it at right angles, looking west, on which the Holy Bible should be placed, and then the minister will only require to turn half round in order to face, in reading the lessons, the great body of his congregation.

The third distinct service is that of the Holy Communion, which was intended to be, and originally was, performed at some considerable interval after the Morning Prayer, allowing the minister time to converse with those who had signified their names as intending to communicate and to call and advertise any of them who should be open and notorious ill-livers or who had done any wrong to their neigh-

[12]Bishop Feild adds the following note: "A short time before this charge was delivered, the pulpit, reading pew and clerk's desk had stood in the middle passage, immediately in front of the Communion table and, being a large and lofty pile, very much obstructed the view towards the east and threw all the services of the Holy Table into the shade. The pulpit is now placed against a pillar on the south side and an open praying desk opposite to it. A stand for the Holy Bible, from which the lessons are read, is placed in the middle passage. The space within the Communion-rails has been considerably enlarged, and the singers have been brought down from a western gallery and placed in two seats on each side of the passage, between the reading desk and Communion-rails on one side and the pulpit and rails on the other, as in most cathedrals. A capacious stone font has, for the first time, been introduced, with decent alms-basins and a silvery flagon for the wine.

[13]See the Order for Morning Prayer.

bours, by word or deed, whereby the congregation might be offended, that they presume not to come to the Lord's Table until they had openly declared themselves to have truly repented and amended their former naughty life. Even this small remnant of discipline seems now to be forgotten or despised.

The union or connection of this service with the Litany is grounded, I presume, upon the same circumstances which I before mentioned as probably causes for saying the Litany in immediate connection with or continuance of the Morning Prayer — viz., the paucity of ministering priests or the dislike, on the part of the congregation, of numerous or multiplied services — causes to be sadly pondered, both of them. But even when more closely connected, as in the present day, a distinction was noted by the practice, which still obtains, of singing before the Communion a psalm or hymn, called originally an introit, because at that time the ministering priest *enters* the chancel or Communion-rails to approach the Holy Table. The very circumstance of passing to another part of the church clearly shows that a fresh or distinct service is about to commence; and I would hope that though we have not in this country the benefit and beauty of the chancel to mark more significantly and impressively the change and advance from a common and open service to that which is ever considered the highest and most sacred of our religion — those holy mysteries, as our Prayer Book calls them — though we have not, I say, the benefit of those chancels, so beautiful and appropriate in all the old churches, I hope you do as far as possible mark the change by going up to and standing as you are directed at the north side of the Holy Table.

And if the service you perform there be, as I have supposed, the highest and most sacred of all, surely it can hardly be necessary to insist upon the inconvenience, not to say indecency, of placing the pulpit and desk immediately in front of the Communion-rails — an intrusion unknown and, I would venture to say, never thought of in any antient church. To what cause this too common but utterly unauthorized innovation may be ascribed I cannot pretend to say, except it be to a preference and exaltation of preaching, not only above prayers but above Communion also. Whether such preference be wise and righteous — for the honour of our Redeemer or the edification of His church — I need not pause to enquire. I would earnestly hope that wherever it be necessary and may be effected without serious inconvenience, some arrangement may be made similar to that adopted or restored in this church: I mean that the pulpit be placed against a side-pillar or side-wall and no longer be allowed to obstruct the view of the Holy Table. It is not the least in my intentions or my thoughts to depreciate the ordinance of preaching or to make it in any way less honourable or acceptable than at present it is in the eyes of our people or to diminish one iota of the care and consideration and study and prayer which you devote to your sermons and discourses from the pulpit: I would rather, if it were necessary and possible, heighten and increase them, but no candid person would suspect me of such designs merely because I would restore the Communion Table and its sacred services and ministering priests to the view and regard of the whole congregation.

I trust I may venture even further without fear of being so misjudged or mistaken and say that though the pulpit is a convenient instrument and contrivance for addressing a congregation, it is by no means the most essential or first requisite in a church. Any clergyman, I conceive, may very fitly and properly preach from the rails of his Communion Table, as was the most antient practice at least in the country churches. And I wish it to be understood that in fitting up or arranging churches, the pulpit should not be considered and provided, as is commonly the case, before the Communion Table with its steps and rails — and for this obvious and sufficient reason that while the sermon may very well be preached from the Communion-steps and rails, the Holy Sacrament cannot at all be administered from the pulpit. I might still further add that the pulpit ought not to be considered and provided even before the font.

From what unhappy necessity the too common omission in this country (for I cannot suppose there is a wilful neglect or indifference about it) of this most necessary and essential instrument and ornament of all Christian churches has arisen I do not exactly know; but I trust you will all endeavour, to the best of your ability, to supply it. You are, no doubt, aware that the canons of our Church require that there should be a font of stone in every church: and it is a well ascertained fact that in all our churches at home the most antient relic is the font of stone — many, I believe, upwards of 800 years old. I need not detain you by detailing the reasons, sufficiently obvious, why the Church has required a font of stone, but it may not be superfluous to remind you that the proper position of the font is near to the west end or principal entrance of the church to instruct us, of course, that by Holy Baptism we enter Christ's church — "are made," so the Catechism declares, "members of Christ, children of God and inheritors of the Kingdom of Heaven." The fonts should be made large enough for immersion because though the Church permits us to pour water upon the child, you will perceive by the rubric that she distinctly recognizes and approves the practice of dipping and directs it to be so done when the sponsors "shall certify that the child may well endure it."

Before I quit the subject of church arrangement, I would beg that, as far as your power or influence may extend, you will always provide that there be one unencumbered and sufficiently wide passage up the centre of the church from west to east, that the seats placed on either side of this passage be all open, without doors or other enclosures, and all ranging one way that the faces of the congregation may be directed towards the upper or east end of the church, that the backs of the seats be so low as not to interrupt the view of any persons looking up to the east from the remotest parts of the building and, particularly and especially, that they be both wide and low enough that all may decently and devoutly kneel. Where people say in the present day that they have a seat or seats in a church, it would have been said formerly that they had so many *kneelings* — a sadly significant change.

Let there be no galleries, except where absolutely necessary for accommodation. Let there be sufficient and ample space round or about the font for the sponsors to stand and kneel and, in like manner, about the Communion-rails and between the rails and Holy Table (until we are blessed with proper chancels) for the solemn preparation and administration of the sacred elements. It is desirable, in most cases, that the rails should run across the whole width of the church from the north to the south walls and the Holy Table should be raised two, three or more steps, according to its distance from the western end. The pulpit may stand indifferently on the north or south of the church as may be most convenient (though antient custom inclines us to the north) and the praying-desk either on the same or opposite side, but not facing, as I have shewn, directly to the people.

These directions will appear minute and, I fear, tedious but cannot by any pious persons be judged unnecessary or unimportant, having regard to the subject and purposes to which they relate: and if we look into the directions which God, almighty and all-wise, Himself gave for the service and furniture of the tabernacle, these are far more minute, numerous and particular, not less so, it has been observed (and why should they be?), than the spots on the wings of an insect or the streaks and colours of a flower. My meaning is that God, who has taken such abundant care (if we may presume to speak so) that there should be order and arrangement and beauty in all the works of His hands, which he pronounced "very good" and which all praise Him, will not be displeased, nay, rather expects and requires of us (having also sufficiently declared His will in this regard by express revelation) that we provide, according to our ability, for a similar accuracy and propriety, even in the minutest parts and circumstances of His worship.

The proper position of the singers is clearly at the upper or east end of the church. You are, no doubt, aware that the chancel is intended for the choir as well as for the ministering priests — they together performing or leading the service, which the congregation below may hear and follow — and nothing can be more foreign to the spirit and purposes of our service than that the congregation should turn and gaze at certain professional performers in a gallery. Singers, as such, not being recognized in our prayer books, you are at liberty to make what arrangements you think most suitable and conducive to the work of solemn and united praise as to their position in the church, number, instruments of music, tunes &c.; and you will, I trust, see reason to regulate their performances and place, as nearly as possible by the antient and best models, taking care that their instruments and tunes be such as suit a church and church-worship.

With respect to the metrical version of psalms and hymns, I desire none other than the old and new versions with the hymns printed in our Books of Common Prayer — and where already introduced, I object not to the psalms and hymns authorized by the American branch of the Episcopal Church. If any other have been introduced or used, I beg they may be discontinued and laid aside. By a judicious selection from the old and new versions, you will be enabled, I think, to meet all the common occasions of praise and thanksgiving in the Church and will avoid the bold and irregular flights and indecent familiarities, not to mention graver errors of speech and doctrine, of too many modern effusions.

We cannot, I fear, have much regard in our present wooden edifices for the symbolism of antient churches, where the minutest ornaments had their peculiar and appropriate significance; but a chancel might, I conceive, be frequently added at very small cost, and the windows generally should be both smaller and higher than I have commonly seen them. Let it be remembered that the design of church-windows is not that passers-by may gaze in or that the congregation may look out but merely that light sufficient for our services may be provided; and I need scarcely say how convenient as well as appropriate it is that this light should descend upon us, as it were, from above. The roofs of our churches may be made with advantage of a sharper pitch and so will be not only more pleasing to the eye but stronger and press less heavily upon the walls and the inside timbers, being a little better finished and ornamented may be left open with very good effect.

I must not omit to draw your particular attention to the sacred vessels, which should always be (the cup and paten at least) of silver, and to purchase these a special collection or collections (in default of any person desiring to present them) should at the earliest opportunity be made. To no other pious object, I conceive, could the alms at the Offertory be more properly be devoted. While almost every private house is furnished with some vessels or ornaments of silver, I will not easily believe but that every congregation might and would provide, at least, a silver paten and cup for their common use at the Lord's Table in the Lord's House — I say at least a paten and cup because we ought not, I think, to be satisfied till the alms-basin and flagon are of the same pure material, remembering, I say, for whose house and service they are provided.

I feel satisfied there is no occasion that should I instruct or remind you that in conducting the prayers and praises of the Church (whether with or for our people) we stand and act between God and them, we present ourselves and them, as it were, at the very gates of heaven and foot-stool of God's throne. With what awe and reverence, with what regard even to outward appearance and behaviour — and still more to inward thoughts, feelings and affections — should we appear in such a presence and engage in such an errand. Nothing can be too serious and earnest and holy, I mean in our thoughts and affections, as to be above what the reason and propriety, not to say the necessity, of such a case requires. Now if the mind be really and devoutly intent upon the duty and service in which we are engaged, it will be affected differently according to the different employment and business in hand — I mean differently in confessing, differently in praying, differently in saying or singing the psalms. This difference, if really felt, will appear naturally and almost necessarily in corresponding ways of utterance and tones of voice.

There will be little room, then, as I am sure there is no occasion, for that wretched mistake of *giving effect*, as it is said, to our admirable liturgy by studied pauses or sudden depressions or elevations of voice or loud, sonorous intonations as if it were the recital of some piece to please or move our congregation instead of a solemn and earnest address to our God and Father. I speak especially now of our prayers and praises, including all the psalms and hymns of the Church — and the same very nearly may be said of the creeds, which are not so much read or repeated for the instruction of the people as devoutly to recite even before God himself the great verities of our Christian faith and hope. Apply these remarks to the Athanasian Creed and it takes off an objection sometimes ignorantly urged against it — viz., that being, as it is supposed, an explanation of certain high and holy mysteries, it is itself full of difficulties. I apprehend, however, that it is not read, or rather said, so much in explanation as in declaration of those great truths which the Church has drawn from or established on Holy Writ, over and for which her confessors and martyrs have studied and prayed and wept and died. And, surely, such considerations will produce a far different feeling and occasion a correspondent difference of expression than if we should consider ourselves reading a lesson or reciting our own feeble discourses.

I am not aware of any variations in the manner of saying the Litany which call for any notice except that I do not know upon what authority we insert a special petition, as it is sometimes done, for those who desire the prayers of the congregation, though as the practice prevails so generally and with such good effect I am not prepared to condemn it.

The Litany ended, is sung the introit or psalm upon the going up of the minister to the Holy Table, and then commences the third service, viz., as I have said, of the Holy Communion. I have supposed that every clergyman will attend to the direction to stand on the north side of the Holy Table, as well as to the other rubrics in that service, among which this one requires our notice, that "nothing shall be proclaimed or published in the Church during Divine Service but by the Minister," which I should be glad to have extended to the psalms and hymns to be sung by the congregation, the Minister giving out and reading each verse to prevent mistakes and assist those who have no books. After the notices, or, if there be none, immediately after the Creed follows the sermon or one of the homilies: and here we must remark that there appears no authority (except that of common practice, if not common consent) for introducing either a psalm or any additional prayers before the sermon.

I am aware, of course, of the canon which prescribes the Bidding Prayer before sermons, but I apprehend that refers only to the occasions, formerly frequent, when sermons were preached without the liturgy, as at the public crosses, in the university churches or cathedrals and many other places. The practice of making or using other prayers before the sermon arose, I imagine, in an evil time and was adopted by perverse and self-righteous men to introduce their own conceits and fancied improvements.[14] After the Restoration, the license was reduced to a collect and the Lord's Prayer; but, the collect not being prescribed, leave is still taken to use this or that, or none, or introduce some extemporaneous or original petitions. I am not bold enough to condemn a practice so common and, I conclude, acceptable, but I confess my own feeling to be that in this, as in other points, the rubric is our best and safest guide and that we should pass with greater propriety immediately from the Nicene Creed to the sermon or homily. For a psalm in this place there is no authority, and it comes in inconveniently when we consider that the Nicene Creed has just been sung or said, which the Church, I have remarked, regards rather or uses in our service in the light of a holy hymn.[15]

The proper prayer after the morning sermon (concluded, of course, with an ascription when our congregations should be instructed to stand) is that "for the whole state of Christ's Church militant here in earth," preceded by the Offertory or sentences to be said by the priest at the Lord's Table, who for that purpose is directed to return thither either, it may be, from the pulpit or the Communion-rails. But here, again, I am aware that long custom has almost grown into a rule and law that the whole service, except when the Holy Communion is administered, should end with the sermon and some collect or collects at the discretion of the minister. I would only, then, venture to recommend that the more antient and authorized mode of returning to the Lord's Table and saying the Offertory and Prayer for the Church Militant be generally adopted in new churches, in others with great caution and consideration. After the Prayer for the Church Militant we are directed, if there be no Communion, to use one or more of the collects at the end of the Communion Service, concluding with the Blessing.

Among the notices which the Curate — i.e., the ministering parish priest — is to give after the Nicene Creed you will find that he is particularly directed to "declare unto the people what Holy-Days or Fasting-Days are in the Week following to be observed." I need hardly tell you it is my wish this rubric should be punctually obeyed; but I draw your attention to it because I have remarked that in some churches where the holy-days are mentioned, and even kept by their proper and appointed public services, the fasting-days are passed over in silence. Now, surely, none can suppose that any branch of the Church — and, I might perhaps say, least of

[14]Bishop Feild writes in a footnote, "The following remarks in a letter from Archbishop Laud to the Vice-Chancellor of Oxford (published in his autobiography) seem to refer to the prayer before sermon: 'That Greenwood who preached on Sunday last is like to prove a peevish man; which I am the more sorry for, because you write he is a good master of his pen, and therefore like to do the more harm. But since he hath so cunningly carried it, for the fashion is now to turn the libelous part into a prayer, &c'."

[15]Bishop Feild adds in a footnote, "These remarks do not apply to the sermon in the afternoon, which, being no part of the appointed service, may properly be preceded by a prayer or collect and concluded in the usual way."

all our own — is entitled and in a condition to keep holy-day with feast and festival without any corresponding seasons of fast and humiliation and repentance.

As little can it be supposed that people do not need to be reminded of those fasting-days and their duties, the evidences to the contrary are, alas! too manifest. Feast and festival — though little, perhaps, according to the will of God and the directions of the Church — feast and festival everywhere; but where are the signs of afflicting ourselves or mourning for our sins or of remembering Christ's sufferings or of renouncing, even for a season, the vanities of a perishing world? It cannot, then, but seem inconsistent or inconsiderate, to use the mildest terms, to begin with restoring feasts and festivals when, both for the Church and ourselves, there is so much more occasion and far greater need of fasting and abstinence, sorrowing and self-abasement. You are all, no doubt, aware that there is in prayer books "a Table of the Days of Fasting and Abstinence, to be observed in the Year," following and in immediate connection with the "Table of Feasts and Holy-Days," and of all these notice should be given in due course on the Sunday when any of them occur on the week following.

It is, of course, desirable, if I should not rather say necessary, to follow up this notice by using the services appointed in our prayer books — I mean particularly for the Saints' Days, the Monday and Tuesday in Easter and Whitsun Week, Ash-Wednesday and all the days of Passion Week — and let us not be deterred from a plain and, I hope I may add, a delightful duty, however much we may be grieved by the thinness of our congregations. Whether it be that numbers cannot or whether it be that they will not join us in those holy services of thanksgiving and praise or of repentance and humiliation, there is surely the more reason that those few who are willing and able should unite their prayers as well for their absent brethren — absent it may be only in body — as for themselves, remembering the encouragement of our Lord's most gracious promise, "Where two or three are gathered together in My name, there will I be in the midst of them."

I will now add a few words on the Occasional Services, among which we may reckon, first of all, the remaining portion of what I have called the third Morning Service, that of Holy Communion. You will, no doubt, have observed that no direction is given as to the time when those who do not communicate should depart and leave the church. Of this apparent omission two explanations may be offered — one that the Holy Communion being formerly a separate as well as distinct service, it was supposed that none but communicants would attend it. Such is actually the case where, on high festivals such as Christmas and Easter, the Communion Service is used by itself in populous places to divide and so lessen the numbers each time. It is common at those festivals, in the large towns in England, to administer the Holy Communion with the proper service singly and separately at 8 o'clock, as well as afterwards in the usual course of the Morning Prayers — and when none but communicants attend, there is no occasion that any should depart; and this would be a probable explanation of the seeming omission. Or the Church may purposely have omitted any directions about departure, using a wise and pious caution lest she might appear to sanction or allow it.

However, so it now is, that the Communion Service is no longer, or very seldom, used separately and distinctly, and many attend the commencement of it who have made no preparation and feel no inclination to communicate. And the question forces itself upon us, When shall these depart? In the absence of any positive directions, custom and the antient services seem to authorize and require their departure at the same time as on other days when there is no Communion — that is, where the Prayer for the Church Militant is commonly read — after that prayer or otherwise as usual after the sermon. I am aware that the custom has of late begun to prevail of requesting the whole congregation to remain on Communion-days during the recital of the Offertory and the Prayer for the Church Militant and collecting alms from all, a custom which has certainly some obvious and great recommendations, particularly in increasing the amount of contributions for pious and charitable purposes and, it may be hoped, enlarging the hearts as well as opening the hands of the brethren towards the Church and her poorer members by the recital of those earnest appeals on this behalf from Holy Writ.

There is, however, or may be one inconvenience attending it, which, as it involves a principle of some importance should, I think, be known and considered — I mean the tendency of it to make people think much of their contributions and little of the sin of turning their backs on the Holy Supper when their alms are received and presented with those of the communicants. I do not say that we must wait and refuse contributions for the Church or poor till we can accomplish it, but surely what we should desire and aim at is to persuade our people that it is a privilege to be allowed to give, specially granted and extended to those who can draw near with faith and take that Holy Sacrament to their comfort. In any case, the alms collected, whether from the whole congregation or communicants only, must be "reverently brought to the Priest, who shall humbly present and place them on the Holy Table."

"When there is a Communion the Priest shall then place upon the Table so much Bread and Wine as he shall think sufficient." I do not know that there is any reason to suppose any variations from the directions in the rubrics, which (as far at least as they concern the minister) are all plain and explicit enough till we come to what is sometimes called the delivery, when the minister is directed to say those solemn words, "The body of our Lord Jesus Christ, which was given for thee, preserve thy body and soul unto everlasting life." Now the rubric directing the use of these words and the words themselves sufficiently and plainly shew that they should be used and addressed separately and singly to each communicant. The rubric says, "When the Minister delivereth the Bread to any one he shall say, 'The body of our Lord Jesus Christ, which was given for thee'. And the Minister that delivereth the Cup to any one shall say, 'The blood of our Lord Jesus Christ, which was shed for thee'." Can the import, I pray, of any words be more solemn or more precise than of these? Upon what pretext, then, can any minister presume to alter both the action and the words and, delivering to two or more persons at once, to say, "The body of our Lord Jesus Christ, which was given for you."

I am aware that in the present state of your congregations these remarks may appear superfluous, as directed against a practice to which you are not even tempted. But I may confess an anxiety to anticipate and prevent an evil which, I lament to know, is sometimes excused on other pleas than that of necessity but which, if you will allow me to say so, I never would under any circumstances sanction or countenance. If it should be asked what must be done when the number of communicants is so large that the delivery cannot be made to one and each person without great fatigue and inconvenience both to the communicants and the minister, it would be quite competent and just to answer that this at least must not be done: you must not disobey a plain rubric, you must not alter perhaps the most precise and precious words in the liturgy. And when you know that the alteration has been made not merely for convenience but to obscure or, rather, to avoid the declaration of a cherished doctrine of the Church, you will, I am persuaded, be the more afraid to offend.

The excuse, however, commonly pleaded for this general rather than particular address and delivery is the time consumed in addressing the words and delivering the sacred elements to each one and the consequent inconvenience and fatigue. Now it is very obvious that this excuse might equally extend and apply to the curtailment or mutilation of other portions of the service. If we are at liberty to alter or omit one portion or one sentence because of inconvenience or fatigue, we surely are at liberty to alter or omit any other or others; and what minister or what congregation would plead for or allow such liberty as this? But the question recurs, when the numbers are so large, as we all hope and desire they may be, that one minister is oppressed and exhausted by the service, what is to be done? Now the obvious and, I sincerely think, the only just and lawful answer to that question is that in every such case the number of ministers must be increased. And will it be asserted, or is it to be believed, that a large number of faithful communicants — for that is the case supposed and the only one which requires to be considered — can see their minister sinking under the burden and responsibility of a right and conscientious discharge of his duty to and for them and not provide the remedy and relief for themselves and him?

Then it was not without occasion or necessity that the Church inserted, at her first review of the liturgy, those solemn and almost indignant appeals of [St. Paul] the apostle [1 Corinthians 9]: "If we have sown unto you spiritual things, is it a great matter if we shall reap your worldly things?" "Who goeth a warfare any time of his own cost [charges]?" "Who planteth a vineyard and eateth not of the fruit thereof? or who feedeth a flock and eateth not of the milk of the flock?" "Do ye not know that they who minister about holy things live of the sacrifice and they who wait at the altar are partakers of the altar? Even so hath the Lord also ordained that they which preach the Gospel, should live of the Gospel?" Read these appeals, then, as you are directed, in the ears of your congregations and, with prayer to God, leave the matter in their hands. And I will not readily believe that a large number of communicants, with hearts inflamed with zeal and charity — zeal for God's honour and charity at least for their own souls — large enough to require such assistance, for their own or their minister's sake, will be either unable or unwilling to provide it, rather than see their ministers exhausted or their services abridged and mutilated or be defrauded of their proper and appointed spiritual food and sustenance. If, however, this relief cannot be obtained, I would far rather consent, nay, advise that the sermon on that occasion be indefinitely abridged, to which no particular form or extent is assigned either in canons or rubrics, or that the Morning Prayers be separated from the other services and said at an earlier hour, which I have already shewn to be the antient arrangement, and only altered for general convenience.

The first rubric which calls for notice in the Baptismal Service is that which directs that "Baptisms should not be administered but on Sundays or other Holy-Days, when the most number of people come together, &c." The nature and necessity of the attendance and duties of sponsors are, I doubt not, sufficiently understood and considered — and I have only to direct your attention to the rubric next in order, that "the Godfathers, Godmothers and the people with the Children, must be ready at the Font either immediately after the last Lesson at Morning Prayer or the last Lesson at Evening Prayer, as the Curate, by his discretion, shall appoint — and the Priest coming to the Font (which is then to be filled with pure Water) and standing there, shall say. . . ." It is very obvious that to neglect this direction renders nugatory the purpose and reason given of requiring the baptisms to be performed on the Sundays or Holy-Days; and on this account, and because the direction is plain and express, I would hope that you will, as quickly as possible, restore this service to its proper place and, I will add, its proper dignity if you have thought it expedient hitherto to baptize at any other time. It may be some encouragement to you to know that having served for 16 years as a parish priest, I constantly observed this rule of the Church, to the great edification, I am persuaded, and I believe also to the entire satisfaction of my congregations. And can any service be more interesting or more edifying to all the parties concerned? And what Christian friend or neighbour is not concerned in the reception of new, though infant, members into the congregation of Christ's flock, to be made heirs together with us of the Christian name and hope?

When two or more children are brought to be baptized, the questions should be addressed to the godparents of each separately because each set of persons must make answer in the singular number for each child, and we are not allowed to alter the form of address from "Dost thou in the name of this child?" to "Do ye in the name of these children?" If the godparents certify that the child is weak, which it may be understood all do who bring the child not prepared for immersion, "it shall suffice," the rubric says, "to pour Water upon it" using, of course, the sacred form of words. I draw your attention to this rubric because we rather too frequently hear of sprinkling children in baptism; and some of you, perhaps, without reflecting about it, may have fallen into that very imperfect and, I must add, improper mode of administering this sacrament. When we remember that it is only of the charity of the Church that it "suffices to pour water," we shall hesitate to adopt an action or a word in so sacred and important a rite which the Church nowhere recognizes nor, I may add, allows. Nothing, as I have already remarked, can be trifling or of no importance in such high and sacred concerns — I might say in any of the concerns of religion — but most certainly and chiefly in those two great sacraments which our church has declared "generally necessary to Salvation."

The next of our public occasional services is the Catechism. I would that it were possible (and why is it not possible?) that all the rubrics relating to it or concerned with it should be noted and observed. That which chiefly concerns your practice is the direction that "the Curate of every Parish shall diligently, upon Sundays and Holy-Days, after the second Lesson at Evening Prayer, openly in the Church instruct and examine so many Children sent unto him, as he shall think convenient, in some part of this Catechism." It may not be superfluous to remark that this rubric says "upon Sundays and Holy-Days" but not all Sundays and Holy-Days. You will, therefore, fulfil the letter at least, if not the spirit, of the rule by thus instructing and examining the children on the first or some other Sunday of every month or, as is more commonly done, though by no means so conveniently and profitably, on all the Sundays in Lent.

I am aware that some persons contend that the Sunday Schools and general education have done away the necessity of this direction, if not superseded the direction itself. Such is not my opinion — the necessity, though different, is, I conceive, equally great and equally urgent, except it should so happen that the clergyman himself attend and instruct at the Sunday School. The necessity, in these days, may not be so much to discover, as formerly, what the children have not learnt but what they have — not so much to add as to diminish or not to supply but to correct. I feel as sincere gratitude as any person can do for the gratuitous and valuable services of Sunday School teachers and monitors, but still it must be remembered they are not the curates of the parish, neither yet pastors and teachers — I mean, to whom Christ has given commission and commandment to feed His lambs — and we are still bound, as ever, to examine and instruct them and, of course, according to that order and rule which the Church has prescribed.

And I can hardly conceive any exercise more pleasant or profitable to the Sunday School teachers themselves, and generally to our people, than to hear from their minister's lips the true explanation and application of those simple but sublime truths which the Catechism contains and which are the groundwork of all Christian education. Still further, there is danger in the present day not only that the matter of instruction be altered and attenuated but that instruction itself, from the mode and manner of it, may be treated with but little regard and reverence — an evil which, we trust, might in some measure be corrected by solemnly conducting it in the Church as part and parcel of Divine Service. I am persuaded there is much need of this caution.

With respect to the Solemnization of Matrimony, I will now only express my wish and hope that you may by degrees, and as quickly as possible, bring the parties to be married within the canonical hours. And as in the absence of parishes it is impossible that the banns should be duly published, there will be the greater need of making other enquiries and using all due circumspection, that you be not betrayed into solemnizing matrimony between two parties who, from near affinity or any other cause, cannot lawfully or honourably be joined together. Great shame, if I should not rather say great guilt, must attach to the minister who, neglecting these due and necessary enquiries, "pronounces them to be man and wife together in the name of the Father and of the Son and of the Holy Ghost" who are forbidden to enter that sacred relation by the positive denunciations of God's holy word or the only by one degree less awful and less authoritative prohibitions of parents and lawful guardians. The whole of the prescribed service you, I trust, always read without omission or mutilation, and it would be well if you should be able to remind the newly-married persons of that rubric at the close of the service that "it is convenient they should receive the Holy Communion at the time of the Marriage, or at the first opportunity after their Marriage."

I am not aware of any variation in the Order for the Burial of the Dead which calls for remarks or any doubt or difficulty which can need to be removed or explained.

The Thanksgiving of Women after Childbirth is the only one that remains of the public occasional services — and there is some variation in the time of introducing and using it, which has do doubt arisen from the want of any positive rule and direction. Some introduce it after the Second Lesson, some before and others after the General Thanksgiving — and others again have deferred it till the conclusion of the Morning or Evening Prayers. The most common, and I therefore conclude the most approved time is just before the General Thanksgiving: though some have remarked that the specially ordered acknowledgements, such as that lately on Her Majesty's behalf, are always used after it and have, therefore, with some reason inferred that to be the most correct place for such acknowledgements on common occasions.[16]

It does not seem easy, and happily it is of no great importance to decide which of these two places is the most proper and authentic, before or after the General Thanksgiving, or whether, in fact, either of them is the right and authorized one. My opinion is that it was designed and originally ordered that this service should be used either before the Morning Prayer or between the Order of Morning Prayer and

[16]Bishop Feild adds in a footnote, "It may be remarked also that the General Thanksgiving stands, in our prayer books, before the Thanksgivings upon particular occasions, while, on the other hand, the Collect or Prayer for All Conditions of Men comes after the prayers for particular parties or persons."

the Holy Communion — that so the woman, having made her special thanks and acknowledgements, might be prepared to join the congregation in the general ones and especially to receive Holy Communion. But though such appears to me the most antient and most fitting method, I would by no means press its adoption, contrary to that more common and, I suppose, more approved one, which has the quasi-authority of long consent and observance, no rule of the Church militating against it.

I cannot but hope, my Reverend Brethren, that this examination of our public services and of the most solemn and approved modes of conducting them is neither the least interesting nor least profitable of the many subjects which may have occurred to you as likely to occupy our attention on this important occasion. That it nearly concerns yourselves, your congregations and God's honour there can be no doubt or question if we are right in supposing that the Church is God's house and we are there as His ministering saints and servants and that all, ministers and people, are assembled and engaged chiefly and especially for His worship and praise: "In His temple doth every man speak of His honour [Psalm 29:9]". We must earnestly protest, and to our power diligently and devoutly provide, that our services in the Church be not considered and treated (as sometimes, I fear, they are, even by pious and single-minded Christians) only as means of grace and ways to become religious — all which we thankfully acknowledge they are — but also and especially as acts of religion acceptable to God through Christ.

Viewing and using them in this light, with what awe and reverence, what gratitude and joy shall we come into His courts and fall low on our knees before His footstool! And for the result and effect — if such may be enquired into — surely the balm and blessing of services so regulated and conducted, so loved and honoured, would remain upon our hearts and appear in our lives till our people would gladly and devoutly say, "We will go with you, for God is with you." But let us beware of considering ourselves or men only in our sacred services. Does not the prophet Isaiah testify that on the walls of the heavenly Jerusalem her watchmen are never silent, singing the praises of God day and night; and the holy seraphim, while with their wings they cover their faces in His presence, cry to another, "Holy, Holy, Holy, Lord God of Hosts, the whole earth is full of His glory [Isaiah 6: 2-3]." And when angels and archangels and all the company of Heaven laud and magnify His glorious name, surely it is our honour and privilege that we may thus copy and join in their worship — may antedate our occupations and enjoyments in the heavenly courts, "And learn to love/God only and the joys above."

Bibliography

Akins, Thomas B. *A Brief Account of the Origin, Endowment and Progress of the University of King's College, Windsor, Nova Scotia*. Halifax: MacNab & Shaffer, 1865.

Coffman, Peter. *Newfoundland Gothic*. Québec: Éditions MultiMondes, 2008.

Davies, Richard. *A Sermon Preached in the Chapel of Lambeth Palace at the Consecration of the Right Rev. Edward, Lord Bishop of Newfoundland, on Sunday, April 28, 1844*. London: Rivington, 1844.

Feild, Edward. *Order and Uniformity in the Public Services of the Church, According to the Use of the United Church of England and Ireland: The Substance of a Charge Delivered to the Clergy of the Diocese of Newfoundland by Edward Feild, D.D., Bishop of Newfoundland, at His First Visitation, on the Feast of St. Matthew, 1844*. St. John's: Printed by John W. M'Coubrey, 1844.

———. *A Journal of the Bishop's Visitation of the Missions on the Western and Southern Coast, August and September 1845, with an Account of the Anniversary Meeting of the Church Society Held October 15, 1845*. Church in the Colonies, No. 10. London: Society for the Propagation of the Gospel, 1846.

———. *A Journal of the Bishop's Visitation of the Missions of the Northern Coast in the Summer of 1846*. Church in the Colonies, No. 15. London: Society for the Propagation of the Gospel, 1846.

———. *Journal of the Bishop of Newfoundland's Voyage of Visitation and Discovery on the South and West Coasts of Newfoundland and on the Labrador in the Church Ship "Hawk" in the Year 1848*. London: Society for the Propagation of the Gospel, 1849.

———. *A Visit to Labrador in the Autumn of MDCCCXLVIII by the Lord Bishop of Newfoundland, with a Preparatory Letter by the Lord Bishop of London*. London: Society for the Propagation of the Gospel, 1849.

———. *Journal of a Voyage of Visitation in the "Hawk" Church Ship on the Coast of Labrador and Round the Whole Island of Newfoundland in the Year 1849*. Church in the Colonies, No. 25. London: Society for the Propagation of the Gospel, 1850.

———. *Journal of the Bishop of Newfoundland's Voyage of Visitation on the Coast of Labrador and the North-East Coast of Newfoundland in the Church Ship "Hawk" in the Year 1853*. London: Society for the Propagation of the Gospel, 1854.

———. *Extracts From a Journal of a Voyage of Visitation in the "Hawk", 1859*. London: Society for the Propagation of the Gospel, 1860.

Forde, H.A. "Amongst the Fogs Newfoundland: Edward Feild, 1801-1876," in *Black and White: Mission Stories*. London: Society for Promoting Christian Knowledge, [1880].

Hollett, Calvin. "Resistance to Bishop Edward Feild in Newfoundland,1845-1857, Harbour Buffett : A Case Study." MA thesis, Memorial University of Newfoundland, 2002.

———. "Bishop Edward Feild: A Wedge in Newfoundland Society," *Newfoundland Quarterly*, 98.3 (2005): 34-40.

The Holy Bible. Authorized King James Version. London and New York: Collins' Clear-Type Press, 1928.

Jones, Frederick. "Bishop Feild, A Study in Politics and Religion in Nineteenth-Century Newfoundland." PhD thesis, University of Cambridge, 1971.

Lear, Edward James. "Edward Feild (1801-1876), Ecclesiastic and Educator: His Influence on the Development of Denominational Education in Newfoundland." M.Ed. thesis, Bishop's University, 1986.

O'Neill, Paul. *The Oldest City: The Story of St. John's, Newfoundland*. 2 vols. Erin, Ont.: Press Porcepic, 1975-76

[Pascoe, C.F.] *Classified Digest of the Records of the Society for the Propagation of the Gospel in Foreign Parts, 1701-1892*. London: SPG, 1893.

Sanderson, Sherri. "How HighWas He? The Religious Thought and Activity of Edward Feild, Second Church of England Bishop of Newfoundland (1844-1876)." MA thesis, Memorial University of Newfoundland, 2007.

Senior, Elinor. "Edward Feild," *Dictionary of Canadian Biography* (Toronto: University of Toronto Press, 1972), 10, 278-81.

Spurr, David. *The Rhetoric of Empire: Colonial Discourse in Journalism, Travel Writing and Imperial Administration*. Durham and London: Duke University Press, 1993.

Tucker, H. W. *Memoir of the Life and Episcopate of Edward Feild, D.D., Bishop of Newfoundland, 1844-1876*. London: W.W. Gardner, 1877.

Wix, Edward. *Six Months of a Newfoundland Missionary's Journal, from February to August 1835*. London: Smith, Elder, 1836.

Index

ISER BOOKS

Studies

73 **The Diary of Bishop Edward field in 1844** – Edited by Ronald Rompkey
72 **To Employ and Uplift Them: The Newfoundland Naval Reserve, 1899-1926** – Mark C. Hunter
71 **Folksongs and Folk Revival: The Cultural Politics of Kenneth Peacock's *Songs of the Newfoundland Outports*** – Anna Kearney Guigné
70 **Global Game, Local Arena: Restructuring in Corner Brook, Newfoundland** – Glen Norcliffe
69 **What Do They Call a Fisherman?** – Nicole Gerarda Power
68 **Narratives at Work: Women, Men, Unionization, and the Fashioning of Identities** – Linda Kathleen Cullum
67 **A Way of Life That Does Not Exist: Canada and the Extinguishment of the Innu** – Colin Samson
66 **Enclosing the Commons: Individual Transferable Quotas in the Nova Scotia Fishery** – Richard Apostle, Bonnie McCay, and Knut H. Mikalsen
65 **Cows Don't Know It's Sunday: Agricultural Life in St. John's** – Hilda Chaulk Murray
64 **Place Names of the Northern Peninsula** - Edited by Robert Hollett and William J. Kirwin
63 **Remembering the Years of My Life: Journeys of a Labrador Inuit Hunter** - recounted by Paulus Maggo, edited with an Introduction by Carol Brice-Bennett
62 **Inuit Morality Play: The Emotional Education of a Three-Year-Old** - Jean Briggs
61 **The Marke of Power: Helgeland and the Politics of Omnipotence** - George Park
60 **Literacy for Living: A Study of Literacy and Cultural Context in a Rural Canadian Community** - William T. Fagan
59 **A Time of Reckoning: The Politics of Discourse in Rural Ireland** - Adrian Peace
58 **The People of Sheshatshit: In the Land of the Innu** - José Mailhot
57 **Looking Out for the Lads: Community Action and the Provision of Youth Services in an Urban Irish Parish** - Stephen A. Gaetz
56 **Making a World of Difference: Essays on Tourism, Culture and Development in Newfoundland** - James Overton
55 **Quest for Equity: Norway and the Saami Challenge** - Trond Thuen
54 **Rough Food: The Seasons of Subsistence in Northern Newfoundland** - John T. Omohundro
53 **Voices from Off Shore: Narratives of Risk and Danger in the Nova Scotian Deep-Sea Fishery** - Marian Binkley
52 **Fishing for Truth: A Sociological Analysis of Northern Cod Stock Assessments from 1977 to 1990** - Alan Christopher Finlayson
51 **Predictions Under Uncertainty: Fish Assemblage and Food Webs on the Grand Banks of Newfoundland** - Manuel Do Carmo Gomes
50 **Dangling Lines: The Fisheries Crisis and the Future of Coastal Communities: The Norwegian Experience** - Svein Jentoft
49 **Port O'Call: Memories of the Portuguese White Fleet in St. John's, Newfoundland** - Priscilla A. Doel

48 **Sanctuary Denied: Refugees from the Third Reich and Newfoundland Immigration Policy, 1906–1949** – Gerhard P. Bassler
47 **Violence and Public Anxiety: A Canadian Case** – Elliott Leyton, William O'Grady and James Overton
46 **What is the Indian 'Problem': Tutelage and Resistance in Canadian Indian Administration** – Noel Dyck
45 **Strange Terrain: The Fairy World in Newfoundland** – Barbara Rieti
44 **Midwives in Passage: The Modernisation of Maternity Care** – Cecilia Benoit
43 **Dire Straits: The Dilemmas of a Fishery, The Case of Digby Neck and the Islands** – Anthony Davis
42 **Saying Isn't Believing: Conversation, Narrative and the Discourse of Belief in a French Newfoundland Community** – Gary R. Butler
41 **A Place in the Sun: Shetland and Oil – Myths and Realities** – Jonathan Wills
40 **The Native Game: Settler Perceptions of Indian/Settler Relations in Central Labrador** – Evelyn Plaice
39 **The Northern Route: An Ethnography of Refugee Experiences** – Lisa Gilad
38 **Hostage to Fortune: Bantry Bay and the Encounter with Gulf Oil** – Chris Eipper
37 **Language and Poverty: The Persistence of Scottish Gaelic in Eastern Canada** – Gilbert Foster
36 **A Public Nuisance: A History of the Mummers Troupe** – Chris Brookes
35 **Listen While I Tell You: A Story of the Jews of St. John's, Newfoundland** – Alison Kahn
34 **Talking Violence: An Anthropological Interpretation of Conversation in the City** – Nigel Rapport
33 **"To Each His Own": William Coaker and the Fishermen's Protective Union in Newfoundland Politics, 1908–1925** – Ian D.H. McDonald, edited by J.K Hiller
32 **Sea Change: A Shetland Society, 1970–79** – Reginald Byron
31 **From Traps to Draggers: Domestic Commodity Production in Northwest Newfoundland, 1850–1982** – Peter Sinclair
30 **The Challenge of Oil: Newfoundland's Quest for Controlled Development** – J.D. House
28 **Blood and Nerves: An Ethnographic Focus on Menopause** – Dona Lee Davis
27 **Holding the Line: Ethnic Boundaries in a Northern Labrador Community** – John Kennedy
26 **'Power Begins at the Cod End': The Newfoundland Trawlermen's Strike, 1974–75** – David Macdonald
25 **Terranova: The Ethos and Luck of Deep-Sea Fishermen** – Joseba Zulaika
24 **"Bloody Decks and a Bumper Crop": The Rhetoric of Sealing Counter-Protest** – Cynthia Lamson
23 **Bringing Home Animals: Religious Ideology and Mode of Production of the Mistassini Cree Hunters** – Adrian Tanner
22 **Bureaucracy and World View: Studies in the Logic of Official Interpretation** – Don Handelman and Elliott Leyton
20 **You Never Know What They Might Do: Mental Illness in Outport Newfoundland** – Paul S. Dinham
19 **The Decay of Trade: An Economic History of the Newfoundland Saltfish Trade, 1935–1965** – David Alexander

18 **Manpower and Educational Development in Newfoundland** – S.S. Mensinkai and M.Q. Dalvi
17 **Ancient People of Port au Choix: The Excavation of an Archaic Indian Cemetery in Newfoundland** – James A. Tuck
16 **Cain's Land Revisited: Culture Change in Central Labrador, 1775–1972** - David Zimmerly
15 **The One Blood: Kinship and Class in an Irish Village** – Elliott Leyton
14 **The Management of Myths: The Politics of Legitimation in a Newfoundland Community** - A.P. Cohen
12 **Hunters in the Barrens: The Naskapi on the Edge of the White Man's World** - Georg Henriksen
11 **Now, Whose Fault is That? The Struggle for Self-Esteem in the Face of Chronic Unemployment** - Cato Wadel
10 **Craftsman-Client Contracts: Interpersonal Relations in a Newfoundland Fishing Community** - Louis Chiaramonte
9 **Newfoundland Fishermen in the Age of Industry: A Sociology of Economic Dualism** - Ottar Brox
8 **Public Policy and Community Protest: The Fogo Case** – Robert L. DeWitt
7 **Marginal Adaptations and Modernization in Newfoundland: A Study of Strategies and Implications of Resettlement and Redevelopment of Outport Fishing Communities** - Cato Wadel
6 **Communities in Decline: An Examination of Household Resettlement in Newfoundland** – N. Iverson and D. Ralph Matthews
5 **Brothers and Rivals: Patrilocality in Savage Cove** – Melvin Firestone
4 **Makkovik: Eskimos and Settlers in a Labrador Community** – Shmuel Ben-Dor
3 **Cat Harbour: A Newfoundland Fishing Settlement** – James C. Faris
2 **Private Cultures and Public Imagery: Interpersonal Relations in a Newfoundland Peasant Society** - John F. Szwed
1 **Fisherman, Logger, Merchant, Miner: Social Change and Industrialism in Three Newfoundland Communities** – Tom Philbrook

Papers

29 **Despite This Loss: Essays on Culture, Memory and Identity in Newfoundland and Labrador** – Ursula Kelly and Elizabeth Yeoman
28 **Remote Control: Governance Lessons for and from Small, Insular, and Remote Regions** – Godfrey Baldacchino, Rob Greenwood, and Lawrence Felt
27 **Coasts Under Stress: Policy Reflections** – Rosemary E. Ommer
26 **Power and Restructuring: Canada's Coastal Society and Environment** – Peter R. Sinclair and Rosemary E. Ommer (eds)
25 **The Resilient Outport: Ecology, Economy, and Society in Rural Newfoundland** – Edited by Rosemary E, Ommer
24 **Finding Our Sea Legs: Linking Fishery People and Their Knowledge with Science and Management** – Edited by Barbara Neis and Lawrence Felt
23 **Just Fish: Ethics and Canadian Marine Fisheries** – Harold Coward, Rosemary Ommer, and Tony Pitcher (eds.)
22 **Labour and Working-Class History in Atlantic Canada: A Reader** – David Frank and Gregory S. Kealey (eds.)

21 **Living on the Edge: The Great Northern Peninsula of Newfoundland** – Lawrence F. Felt and Peter R. Sinclair (eds.)
20 **Pursuing Equality: Historical Perspectives on Women in Newfoundland and Labrador** – Linda Kealey (ed.)
19 **Living in a Material World: Canadian and American Approaches to Material Culture** – Gerald L. Pocius (ed.)
18 **To Work and to Weep: Women in Fishing Economies** – Jane Nadel-Klein and Dona Lee Davis (eds.)
17 **A Question of Survival: The Fisheries and Newfoundland Society** – Peter R. Sinclair (ed.)
16 **Fish Versus Oil: Resources and Rural Development in North Atlantic Societies** – J.D. House (ed.)
15 **Advocacy and Anthropology: First Encounters** – Robert Paine (ed.)
14 **Indigenous Peoples and the Nation-State: Fourth World Politics in Canada, Australia and Norway** – Noel Dyck (ed.)
13 **Minorities and Mother Country Imagery** – Gerald Gold (ed.)
12 **The Politics of Indianness: Case Studies of Native Ethnopolitics in Canada** – Adrian Tanner (ed.)
11 **Belonging: Identity and Social Organisation in British Rural Cultures** – Anthony P. Cohen (ed.)
10 **Politically Speaking: Cross-Cultural Studies of Rhetoric** – Robert Paine (ed.)
9 **A House Divided? Anthropological Studies of Factionalism** – M. Silverman and R.F. Salisbury (eds.)
8 **The Peopling of Newfoundland: Essays in Historical Geography** – John J. Mannion (ed.)
7 **The White Arctic: Anthropological Essays on Tutelage and Ethnicity** – Robert Paine (ed.)
6 **Consequences of Offshore Oil and Gas – Norway, Scotland and Newfoundland** – M.J. Scarlett (ed.)
5 **North Atlantic Fishermen: Anthropological Essays on Modern Fishing** – Raoul Andersen and Cato Wadel (eds.)
3 **The Compact: Selected Dimensions of Friendship** – Elliott Leyton (ed.)
2 **Patrons and Brokers in the East Arctic** – Robert Paine (ed.)
1 **Viewpoints on Communities in Crisis** – Michael L. Skolnik (ed.)

Mailing address:
ISER Books
Faculty of Arts Publications
Memorial University of Newfoundland
297 Mount Scio Road
St. John's, Newfoundland
A1C 5S7

Telephone: (709) 864-3453 FAX : (709) 864-4342
email: iser-books@mun.ca
***NEW* Website: http://www.arts.mun.ca/iserbooks**